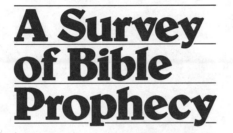

# A Survey of Bible Prophecy

# A Survey
# of Bible
# Prophecy

## R. Ludwigson

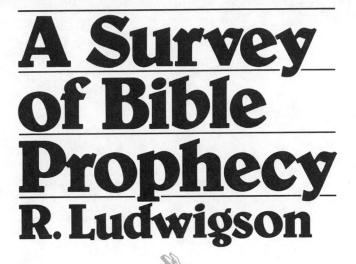

Academie
Books Grand Rapids, Michigan

Zondervan Publishing House

# CONTENTS

# MAPS AND CHARTS

# PREFACE TO THE FIRST EDITION

There have always been, from the early days of the Christian Church, differences of opinion regarding some of the basic doctrines of the Christian faith. Such differences have been evident e.g., in the problem of the actual meaning and significance of the sacraments. The early Church was tormented by various views on the relationship of Christ's deity to His humanity. In modern times, wide differences of opinion have arisen as to the exact meaning of what is called the "inspiration" of the Scriptures. But in no area have these diversities been so many, and so pronounced, as in the area of Biblical prophecy, especially those prophecies which point to events still in the future. Some of the differences here are primary, and some secondary: some color all of one's theological thinking, while others can be locked up in small compartments. A comparatively minor prophetic theme, I would say, is the meaning of Babylon in the prophetic Scriptures, in the Old Testament and the Book of Revelation — yet there are five different fundamental views of what this Babylon might be! There are three different schools of thought regarding the tribulation, and three basic views on the millennium, and the view one finally takes on these subjects will have a tremendous influence over his whole outlook on world events, and his concept of many factors relating to the second advent of our Lord.

It is inevitable that these varied opinions, promoted by men whose writings are rather extensive, whose devotion to the Word of God is never questioned, and whose influence is somewhat marked, should result in confusion for multitudes, and those who would like to come to some convictions concerning many of these topics must confess that they need and seek guidance.

I do not know of any small volume written during the last half-century, which so fairly and clearly presents the different views of these major prophetic themes as does this work by Dr. Ludwigson. It is not an exhaustive treatment of Biblical prophecy, but it is an excellent summary of differing views on the kingdom, the millennium, the tribulation, the restoration of Israel, and the second advent of our Lord, as well as other subjects growing out of these topics. The bibliographies are helpful. Dr. Ludwigson has made a very careful study of much of this literature, and of the Biblical data, and I feel confident that many Bible students in this country will be most grateful to him for having set forth in clear, brief outline form the opinions held by various dependable students of the Word of God, especially in modern times.

It is a pleasure to commend this volume to that increasing number of Christians who love the Scriptures, and who seek to arrive at some convictions of their own regarding these great truths which must be given, and are being given, more and more serious attention as the crisis of our time deepens and the end of the age seems to be drawing near.

WILBUR M. SMITH

*Pasadena, Calif.*

# PREFACE

At the time when the manuscript for the first edition of these notes on prophecy was written, there were no books on prophecy available that presented the varying interpretations of key prophecies of the Bible. The books on prophecy that were available set forth and defended only a single viewpoint, such as a pre-tribulation rapture or a postmillennial kingdom. Therefore, the original motivation for the publishing of these notes was to present as objectively as possible in one book the positions of various schools of thought, so that students of prophecy might be able to examine and weigh the validity of the defense of the varying positions for themselves. Also, the notes were presented in an outline structure to make it easy for the student of Bible prophecy to see at a glance the characteristic aspects of a prophetic theme and also to provide an opportunity for him to add his own subpoints to the outline, should he wish to do so.

Prophetic subjects such as ARMAGEDDON, WORLD CONDITIONS IN THE LAST TIMES, MILLENNIUM, RAPTURE, SECOND COMING OF CHRIST, and THE GREAT TRIBULATION need no explanation as to their right to appear in a book on Bible prophecy. Such titles as the KINGDOM and the CHURCH, however, might need some justification. They find their place in such a study because the arguments used by pre-, mid-, and post-tribulation rapturists for their varying positions, for instance, depend on an understanding and interpretation of the nature and destiny of the Church and the Kingdom.

For the sake of convenience in locating the various subjects, they have been placed in alphabetical order.

R. LUDWIGSON

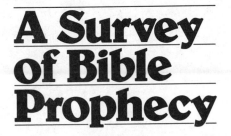

# A Survey of Bible Prophecy

# ANTICHRIST

## Definition

Antichrist, as the two bases of the word indicates, refers to any opponent of Christ. The title in the New Testament, however, refers primarily to the last great adversary against Christ who shall appear in the tribulation period at the end of this age. At that time Antichrist will fill the world with wickedness and finally be destroyed by Christ at His Second Coming.

## Biblical Descriptions of Antichrist

The word "Antichrist" is used in the New Testament only by the Apostle John in his first and second epistles: 1 John 2:18 and 22; 4:3; and 2 John 7. These Bible verses state the following facts about Antichrist:

1. The spirit which characterizes the future Antichrist was at work even in the time of the Apostle John.

2. Antichrist is expected in the last times (1 John 2:18 and 22; 4:3).

3. The spirit of Antichrist is that of apostasy: "They went out from us, but they were not of us" (1 John 2:19).

4. The spirit of Antichrist is that of a liar denying that Jesus is the Christ. "He is antichrist that denieth the Father and the Son" (1 John 2:22). The word "liar" used here suggests the idea of a false man who breaks faith (Thayer) (cf. Dan. 9:27).

13

5. The spirit of Antichrist is a denial of the Incarnation of Christ: ". . . and every spirit that confesseth not that Jesus Christ is come in the flesh is . . . that spirit of Antichrist" (1 John 4:3; 2 John 7).

While not containing the word "Antichrist," several other Bible passages are interpreted by many Bible teachers to refer to this opponent of Christ who shall appear at the end of the age. In these passages are a number of different names and descriptions of Antichrist:

1. The "little horn" (Dan. 7:7, 8, 20-26);
2. The "prince that shall come" (Dan. 9:27);
3. The "king" (Dan. 11:36-45);
4. The "false Christ" (Matt. 24:24; Mark 13:6, 21, 22; Luke 21:8);
5. The "man of lawlessness"; "son of perdition"; "that lawless one" (2 Thess. 2:8);
6. The "beast out of the sea" (Rev. 11:7; 13:1-10; 17:8-17);
7. The "beast out of the earth" (Rev. 13:11-17).

How many of these eight biblical references may be applied to the future Antichrist is a question about which there is some difference of opinion. Before a passage can be said to refer to the Antichrist, there must be some evidence that the passage describes him and harmonizes with other passages ascribed to him. Thus, the final selection and application of a passage of Scripture not containing the word Antichrist rests upon an interpretation of its contents.

Not every interpretation, however, applies the term Antichrist to an individual. Some interpreters identify the term with a political system; others, with a false religion or teaching.

### A Variety of Interpretations

Various interpretations of the eight passages listed above are as follows:

### 1. The "little horn."

In a vision Daniel the prophet sees four successive beasts coming out of the sea: a lion, a bear, a leopard, and an unnamed beast. The unnamed beast has ten horns among which arises another little horn, the eleventh. The first three beasts represent the three world kingdoms that will arise: Babylon, Medo-Persia, and Greece. The fourth and unnamed beast represents the kingdom that will be in existence when the Ancient of Days appears. The ten horns of this unnamed beast represent ten kings who will arise to rule the kingdom. An eleventh horn or king finally appears and overcomes three of the ten kings. Four specific statements identify the eleventh little horn (Dan. 7:11, 12; 24-26):

a. He speaks great words against the Most High.
b. He persecutes the saints.
c. He changes times and laws for a period of three and one-half years.
d. And finally, he will be slain by the direct judgment of God; his body will be burned; and his kingdom will be destroyed.

Because this little horn continues until the coming of the Ancient of Days, and because his description is similar to that of the man of sin in 2 Thessalonians 2, who will be revealed just before the day of Christ, this eleventh little horn has been identified as the Antichrist of the end time.

### 2. The "prince that shall come."

The prince that shall come will make a covenant with Daniel's people for one week. In the middle of the week, the prince will break the covenant and set up the abomination of desolation (possibly the image referred to in Revelation 13:14, 15). Finally, a predetermined destruction will be poured upon the prince at the end of the seventy weeks.

> And a stringent statute shall be issued against the many for one week; And so for the first half of the week the

sacrifice and the meat offering shall cease: and in the stead shall be a horror that appalleth; and that until the annihilation that is already determined shall be poured out upon the desolator (Dan. 9:27). (As translated by R. H. Charles, *Commentary on Daniel*).

Christ said that Daniel's prophecy would be fulfilled just before His Second Coming (Matt. 24:15). He added that the setting up of the "abomination of desolation" would introduce a period of tribulation unequaled in history. Because Christ referred the fulfillment of Daniel's prophecy to the future when He would return, the "prince" of Daniel 9:27 has been identified with the Antichrist of end times.

For a further discussion of the time, see DANIEL'S SEVENTY WEEKS to follow.

3. *The "king."*

The passage in which this epithet of Antichrist appears is manifestly difficult (Dan. 11:36-45). The problem lies in the selection of verses which may be applied to the end time as over against the portion of the chapter that reveals an earlier historical fulfillment in the time of Antiochus Epiphanes, 165 B.C. Four views held by Bible teachers are as follows:

a. The entire chapter speaks of the successors of Alexander in Syria and Egypt, up to the end of the reign of Antiochus Epiphanes (Historical-Critical School).

b. The first part of the chapter (Dan. 11:1-20) applies to the Ptolomies and the Seleucids; the second part (Dan. 11:21-45) gives the closing events of Israel's history in the time of the end when Antichrist reigns (Jerome).

c. The first part (vv. 1-20) gives the history of Alexander the Great's successors; the middle section (vv. 21-32) tells of the reign of the Seleucid king, Antiochus the Great. A break at verse 33 introduces a prophecy of the time of the end. Verse 36 prophesies specifically of Antichrist (B. W. Newton, the Scofield Bible).

d. Verses 5-20 relate the condition of the kingdoms of

Syria and Egypt *just prior* to the rise of Antichrist. Verses 21-45 give the history of one person at *the time of the end*. A long interval of time exists between verses 4 and 5 ( S. P. Tregelles).

As mentioned above in 3c, the Scofield Bible refers the description of "the king" in Daniel 11:36-45 to the "little horn" of Daniel 7, i.e., to the Antichrist of the end time. Accordingly, the following facts applicable to the Antichrist may be gleaned from Daniel 11:36-45:

(1) The king will do according to his own will.

(2) He will exalt himself above every god, speaking against the God of gods. He will disregard the God of his fathers and the desire of women. (Some have interpreted this to mean that the Antichrist would be a Jew who apostatized from the faith of the patriarchs: Abraham, Isaac, and Jacob. He does not regard the Messiah as the King whom the Jewish women desired to bring into the world. Others, however, have interpreted his disregard of the desire of women as a moral offense against womanhood itself, interpreting the "desire of women" as the inherent desire for human love.)

(3) He will honor the god of forces or of military strength.

(4) He will be opposed by the king of the South and by the king of the North.

(5) He will enter Palestine, and he will overthrow many countries; however, Edom, Moab, and Ammon will escape. With Libya and Ethiopia as his allies, he will overthrow Egypt.

(6) Rumors from the East and the North will trouble him. These rumors have been interpreted as tidings of revolt among the people. He will seek to quell the revolt.

(7) He will be destroyed and none will help him.

Since this king has power at the time that Michael stands up for Daniel's people (Dan. 12:1; cf. Rev. 12:7), and at the time when there will be unparalleled trouble (Dan. 12:1), and also until the time of the resurrection (Dan.

12:1, 2); this passage (Dan. 11:36-45) has been applied to the Antichrist of the end times.

4. *"False Christ."*

The passages in the gospels containing "false Christ" do not refer directly to a particular Antichrist. They warn of pseudo-Christs and false prophets who will arise and deceive many (cf. Matt. 24:11). These false leaders will do great signs and wonders which, if possible, would deceive even the elect.

5. *"The man of lawlessness"; "son of perdition"; "that lawless one."*

This passage presents the following facts concerning the revelation of Antichrist:

a. He will not be revealed until after the "falling away" comes. Two events will precede the Second Coming of Christ: the falling away and the revealing of the "man of lawlessness, the son of perdition." These two specific prophecies were given to the Thessalonian church to forestall undue speculation and anxiety.

The definite article, used in the Greek text, specifies the first happening as "*the* falling away." The Greek root of "falling away" is sometimes translated in the New Testament as "depart." Hence, the passage has been interpreted as: (1) the "falling away" from the faith, as used in 1 Timothy 4:1 to describe a condition of *apostasy* of the last times; or (2) as a "departing," or rapture, of the church before the day of Christ. This would then be in accord with the statement in verse 7 (see 2e below).

b. He will be called the "son of perdition." The "son of perdition" means literally "son of destruction." Since Judas Iscariot is also referred to as the "son of perdition" (John 17:12), some have advanced the view that Judas may be resurrected to become the Antichrist at the end of the age.

c. He will oppose God and exalt himself as God.

d. His spirit will be one of lawlessness and iniquity,

which is already at work in the world even in the writer's day (about 51 A.D.).

e. He will not come until the hinderer, or restrainer, is removed. The restrainer, or that which "withholdeth" (2 Thess. 2:6) is neuter, i.e., some definite *thing* will be taken out of the way before the Antichrist is revealed. In verse 7, however, the restrainer, or "he that will be taken out of the way," is masculine and would refer literally to some *person* or individual who withholds or hinders the revelation of Antichrist. The expression, "be taken out of the way," is literally "will be out of the midst," and the word "withholdeth" literally means "to hold fast." The most outstanding interpretations of the identity of the restrainer are as follows:

(1) The Holy Spirit.

Since the work of the Holy Spirit is to convict men of sin, iniquity cannot come into full fruition until His removal. The restraining *thing* would then be the work of the Holy Spirit, and the restraining *person*, the Holy Spirit Himself.

(2) The Church.

Since the Holy Spirit abides in the believer, the Church or the body of believers in a sense exercises a restraining influence in checking lawlessness and iniquity.

(3) Human Government or Civil Power.

Since civil government strives to maintain some measure of law, order, and righteousness; the lawless iniquity of the Antichrist could not come into existence until the restraining influence of orderly and righteous civil government be removed.

Some of the early Church Fathers held this view with respect to the Roman Empire. Later interpreters modified the "hinderer" to be the restraining power of human law, not by one government, but by the many governments of the civilized world.

(4) The Determinate Counsel of God.

According to this view Antichrist will not appear until the time predetermined in the mind of God. This view was first held by Theodore of Mopsuestia (350 A.D.).

It is interesting to note that the Early Church Fathers agreed that the prophecy of 2 Thessalonians 2 had not yet been fulfilled in their day. They concurred in the interpretation of the man of sin as a real person, as the very personification of sin — the Antichrist, who would be judged by the personal return of the Lord Jesus Christ when He comes to set up His kingdom.

Since this lawless one continues until the coming of the Lord, and is destroyed by the brightness of His coming, this lawless one has been identified as the Antichrist of the end time.

### 6. The "beast out of the sea."

Two beasts are to arise in the end times; one, out of the sea; the other, out of the earth. Concerning "the beast out of the sea," the following facts are revealed:

a. He rose out of the sea. According to Revelation 17:15, the sea represents the nations of the world out of which this final ruler arises.

b. He had seven heads and ten horns. The seven heads are seven mountains which symbolize seven kings dominated by the Harlot Babylon (Rev. 17:9). Five of these kings have fallen, the sixth is reigning, and the seventh has not yet come at the time in the tribulation period that John is describing. When the seventh king comes, he will continue "a little while" (Rev. 17:10). The beast will follow the reign of these seven; he is the eighth in succession, but actually is one of the seven who comes to power again after a deadly wound has healed.

The ten horns (Rev. 17:12) are ten kings who will receive power and authority together with the beast out of the sea (cf. Rev. 13:1-10 and Rev. 17:8, 11). They will rule together for one hour just before they make war on the Lamb — evidently the battle of Armageddon (Rev. 19:

17-21). The beast along with the false prophet is finally captured and thrown alive into the lake of fire that burns with brimstone. All this takes place at the end of the reign of the beast who rules for the final three and a half years of this present age.

The Harlot Babylon (Rev. 17:8) is the great city which will have dominion over the seven kings, as suggested figuratively by the woman sitting upon the seven mountains. The ten kings, together with the beast, will war against this great city which they will destroy and burn with fire (Rev. 17:16). This destruction of Babylon will occur at the close of the tribulation period when the seventh and last bowl of the wrath of God is poured out upon the earth (Rev. 16:17-20).

c. Upon his head were names of blasphemy. The seven kingdoms are blasphemous against God. The final ruler, the beast who is of the seven, for instance, openly blasphemes against God, against His dwelling, and against those who dwell in heaven.

d. He was like a leopard, a bear, and a lion. These descriptions allude to those given by Daniel in reference to ancient world empires. Here the allusions suggest that the final world dominion of Antichrist will resemble in substance former world empires.

e. His power, his throne, and his authority were given to him by "the dragon," which is identified later as Satan (Rev. 12:9), who bestows on the beast his own destructive power.

f. One head was wounded and healed. The seven heads are seven kings, or kingdoms, one of which suffered a mortal wound, but healed again. One king or kingdom, thus, ceases for a time, but rises again into reigning power.

g. The beast continues for forty-two months, the period of the time of the end, or of the great tribulation.

h. He wars with the saints and overcomes them.

i. He is given power over all nations.

j. He ascends out of the bottomless pit. As a person,

the beast comes up out of the sea, i.e., out of the nations of the world. As energized by Satan, from whom also he receives his power, the beast comes from the bottomless pit.

k. His number is 666, perhaps the symbol of man's greatest strength, but also symbolic that he is only a man.

l. He kills the two witnesses in Jerusalem who, accompanied by supernatural power, evangelize in the end times (Rev. 11:7).

m. He is destroyed by the Lamb, goes into perdition, and is finally cast into the lake of fire (Rev. 19:20).

The first beast has also been identified with the little horn of Daniel:

| "Little horn" (Daniel 7) | First "beast" (Revelation 13) |
|---|---|
| 1. The beast whose power is absorbed into the little horn has ten horns (Dan. 7:7). | 1. The beast has ten horns (Rev. 13:1). |
| 2. Rises from the sea (Dan. 7:3). | 2. Rises from the sea (Rev. 13:1). |
| 3. Has mouth speaking great things (Dan. 7:8). | 3. Same (Rev. 13:5). |
| 4. Makes war with saints and prevails (Dan. 7:21). | 4. Makes war with saints and overcomes them (Rev. 13:7). |
| 5. Speaks great words against Most High (Dan. 7:25). | 5. Opens mouth in blasphemy against God (Rev. 13:6). |
| 6. Wears out saints of Most High (Dan. 7:25). | 6. Woman, who rides on beast and directs him, is drunken with blood of saints (Rev. 17:6). |

7. *The "beast out of the earth."*

The second beast is described as follows:

a. He causes the people of the earth to worship the first beast.

b. He works miracles.

c. He deceives the people.

d. He causes the image of the first beast to be erected.

e. He kills all who refuse to worship the image.

f. He brands all who worship the first beast.

g. He denies civil liberties to those who refuse to worship the first beast.

Two general opinions prevail at the present time as to which of the two beasts in Revelation 13 is the Antichrist: (1) the first beast of Revelation 13 is considered to be the civil or political leader of the last world empire, while the second beast or false prophet is considered to be the last ecclesiastical leader of the apostate church and the Antichrist (The Scofield Bible, Arno Gaebelein, H. A. Ironside, F. W Grant, William Lincoln, and Walter Scott); and (2) the first beast of Revelation 13 is the civil or political leader known as the Antichrist of the end time, and the second beast or false prophet is his assistant (William R. Newell, William Pettingill, I. M. Haldeman, Joseph Seiss, William G. Moorhead, Ford C. Ottman, J. Dwight Pentecost, Donald Grey Barnhouse, and Hal Lindsey).

### Summary

On the supposition that the above verses refer to Antichrist, the following statements can be made about the Antichrist of end times:

1. *His Origin and Person.*

a. He will be the eleventh king who will arise from among ten last contemporary world kingdoms, which will exist immediately preceding our Lord's return to earth.

b. He will come up from the bottomless pit, that is, he will be energized by Satan himself; he will be called the "son of perdition."

c. He will be a proud and arrogant individual who is characterized by the spirit of lawlessness.

d. Disregarding the god of his fathers, he will speak blasphemous things against God and against all that is called God. He will set himself forth as god to receive worship.

2. *His Work.*

a. He will set up the abomination of desolation in the temple.

b. He will change times and laws.

c. He will honor the god of forces and exercise world authority.

d. He will oppose the Lamb.

e. He will make a covenant with Israel for one week and break it in the middle of the week.

f. He will kill the two witnesses in Jerusalem and persecute the saints.

g. Three of the ten last world kingdoms he will overthrow.

h. Along with Libya and Ethiopia as allies, he will overthrow Egypt, the king of the South.

i. He will enter the glorious land, Palestine.

j. With the help of ten kings at the very end of the period, he will destroy the great city, Mystery Babylon, that bears rule over the kings of the earth.

k. Immediately preceding Christ's second coming, he will gather together the kings of the earth at Armageddon to war against Christ Himself.

3. *His Time.*

a. He will be revealed when that which "withholdeth" is removed.

b. He will be given power and authority for a period of three and a half years at the end of the tribulation period.

4. *His Judgment.*

The Antichrist will be destroyed by the appearing of Christ at His Second Coming, and along with the false prophet, will be cast into the lake of fire.

The following table summarizes a brief and select history of various interpretations as to the identity of Antichrist:

| Antichrist is: | Held by: |
| --- | --- |
| Docetism or Gnosticism | Polycarp |
| Rome, the fourth empire of the visions of Daniel | Barnabas |
| Nero to be raised from the dead | Victorinus |
| Roman Catholic Church and the Papacy | Martin Luther and John Calvin |
| Luther and the Protestant Churches | Roman Catholic writers |
| Napoleon | Various writers of that time |
| Nero (Some apply all details to the first century. The Lord revealed from heaven refers to the destruction of Jerusalem. The first resurrection also occurred then.) | Milton Terry on Hermeneutics |
| The beast out of the sea is the Roman Empire (Diocletian) and the beast out of the earth is the Papacy. | E. W. Hengstenberg, Philip Mauro |
| The beast out of the earth is the Romish hierarchy during the time of the Spanish Inquisition (16th Century); fire from heaven is the Inquisition itself. | Adam Clark, Patrick Fairbairn |
| An embodiment of Satan | R. C. Trench |
| The "lawless one" in 2 Thessalonians is a Jewish false Christ, held in check by the Roman Empire. The first beast (Rev. 13) is the restored Roman Empire; the second beast is pseudo-prophecy supporting the first beast. | Bernard Weiss |
| An openly infidel supplanter of the Papacy | A. R. Fausset |

| | |
|---|---|
| Last ecclesiastical head, an apostate from Christianity (Second beast out of the earth) | C. I. Scofield |
| Last ecclesiastical head, an apostate Jew (the beast out of the earth) | H. A. Ironside, Arno C. Gaebelein |
| First beast of Rev. 13 is Antichrist; the second beast is the false prophet who supports him | J. N. Darby, W. R. Newell, also J. Seiss, J. Dwight Pentecost, Donald Grey Barnhouse, Hal Lindsey, W. A. Criswell, who add that it may be Judas Iscariot resurrected |

## Bibliography

Aldrich, Roy L. "The Final Apostasy Identified," *The Sunday School Times*, 97:6 (February 5, 1955).

Barnhouse, Donald Grey. *Revelation: An Expository Commentary*. Grand Rapids, Michigan: Zondervan Publishing House, 1971.

Criswell, W. A. *Expository Sermons on Revelation*. Grand Rapids, Michigan: Zondervan Publishing House, 1962.

Darby, J. N. *Notes on the Apocalypse*. London: G. Morrish, no date.

Elliott, Russell. "The Antichrist," *Our Hope*, 54:335-38 (December, 1948).

Gaebelein, Arno C. *The Prophet Daniel*. New York: Our Hope, 1911.

Hogg, C. F., and Vine, W. E. *The Epistle of Paul the Apostle to the Thessalonians*. Glasgow: Pickering and Inglis, 1914.

Ironside, H. A. *Lectures on the Revelation*. New York: Loizeaux Brothers, no date.

Jennings, F. C. *Studies in Revelation*. New York: Loizeaux Brothers, 1950.

Kelly, William. *The Revelation Expounded*. London: F. E. Race, no date.

Lincoln, William. *Lectures on the Book of Revelation*. New York: Fleming H. Revell, no date.

Moorhead, William G. *Studies in the Book of Revelation*. Pittsburgh: United Presbyterian Board orf Publication, 1908.

Rae, William G. "The Two Beasts of Revelation," *Our Hope*, 54:14-18 (July, 1947).

Scott, Walter. *Exposition of the Revelation of Jesus Christ*. London: Pickering and Inglis, no date.

Seiss, Joseph. *The Apocalypse*. Grand Rapids: Zondervan Publishing House, 1900.

Stevens, W. C. *Revelation, the Crown-Jewel of Prophecy*. New York: Christian Alliance Publishing Company, 1928.

# ARMAGEDDON

## Definition

Armageddon will be the final cataclysmic battle at the very end of the tribulation period when the kings of the earth, under Antichrist, will gather together to invade Israel and to war against the King of Kings, the Lord Jesus Christ. The future struggle of Armageddon has been called the battle of God Almighty (Rev. 16:14). The armies will be gathered from the land of the sunrising to cross the dried up River Euphrates (Rev. 16:12-16). They will be gathered by unclean spirits at the command of the beast, the dragon, and the false prophet. These are the armies of the last ten kings that will rule on the earth (Rev. 17:3, 14). They have joined with the Antichrist and rule in a confederacy of power for a very brief time at the end of this age, immediately before Christ's second coming. They turn against Mystery Babylon, the great city of the end times, and burn it (See BABYLON). Then they turn to fight against the Lord Himself (Rev. 17:14; cf. Rev. 19:11-21). Some Bible teachers identify the invasion of Gog and Magog with the Armageddon battle (See GOG AND MAGOG).

The battle takes its name from the area in Palestine where it will be fought. Armageddon is located in north central Palestine on the southern edge of the plains of Esdraelon, west of the Jordan, about fifteen miles from the Mediterranean coast. Armageddon guards the pass from

Egypt through the Carmel ridge to the valleys of the Euphrates and Tigris Rivers.

The plains of Esdraelon have been the site of several great battles in Old Testament times:

1. The victory of Deborah and Barak over the Canaanites (Judg. 4 and 5).
2. The victory of Gideon over the Midianites (Judg. 7).
3. The death of Saul in the invasion of the Philistines (1 Sam. 31:8).
4. The death of Ahaziah by Jehu (2 Kings 9:27).
5. The death of Josiah in the invasion of the Egyptians (2 Kings 23:29, 30; 2 Chron. 35:22).

### Bible References Concerning the Future Battle of Armageddon

The Bible references concerning the future battle are found in Revelation 16:12-16; 19:19-21; Zechariah 14:1-3; 12:1-6, 9-14; Joel 3:1, 2, 9-17. These verses state the following facts about the future struggle between the angry nations and the Lord.

### 1. *The Reason for Armageddon*

The reason for the battle of Armageddon may be said to be a judgment upon the nations:

a. Because they have scattered Israel and appropriated Israel's land (Joel 3:2);
b. Because of their wickedness (Rev. 16:14; 19:15);
c. Because of their failure to glorify God (Rev. 16:9).

### 2. *The Time of Armageddon*

The battle of Armageddon will take place at the very end of the tribulation period. The time is further specified as:

a. The pouring out of the sixth bowl of God's wrath (Rev. 16:12);
b. The second coming of Christ (Rev. 11:16; Zech. 14:4; Joel 3:15, 16);
c. The time of Israel's regathering (Joel 3:1; Zeph. 3:20).

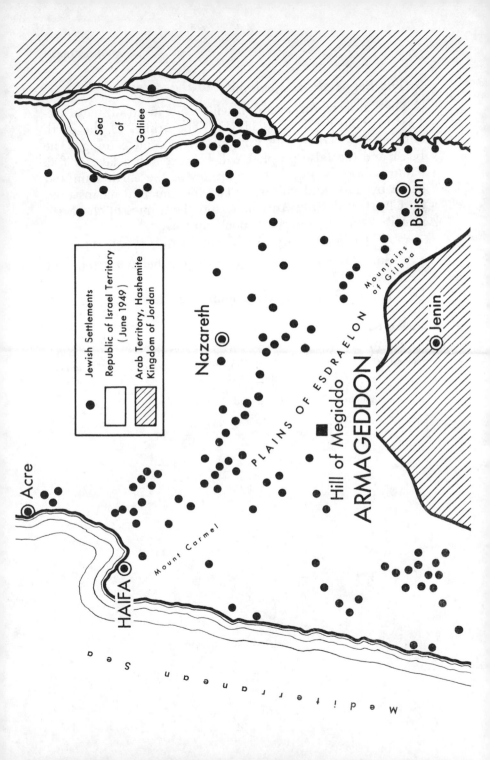

## 3. *The Result of Armageddon*

The battle of Armageddon will result in an ultimate victory for Christ (Rev. 19:11-21). The armies of the earth will be defeated by the Lord at His second coming. The beast and the false prophet will be cast into a lake of fire. Satan will be bound and the armies of the earth slain and eaten by birds and vultures. The instrumental means used by Christ to destroy Antichrist and the armies of the earth at His return is described poetically as:

    a. A plague, causing tumult and mutiny (Zech. 14:2, 3);

    b. Superhuman strength given to the believing remnant (Zech. 12:6);

    c. The brightness of His coming (2 Thess. 2:8, 9).

### Bibliography

Fereday, W. W. "Armageddon," *Our Hope,* 47:397-401 (December, 1940).
Scofield, C. I. "The Last World Empire and Armageddon," *Bibliotheca Sacra,* 108:355-62 (July, 1951).
(Also commentaries on Daniel 9 and Revelation 16, 17 and 19; cf. commentaries on Ezekiel 38 and 39.)

# BABYLON

## Definition

A great commercial city will come into existence during the tribulation period at the end of this age. It is called "Mystery Babylon" (Rev. 17 and 18). It is described as "the great whore," which symbolizes "a great city" (Rev. 17:1, 18). The city is further described as the ruler over the seven last kings of the earth (Rev. 17:18). The kingdom of the Antichrist will be the eighth king, but is actually one of the previous seven who is restored to power (Rev. 17:11). He will be supported by a confederacy of ten kings who will rule with him a very brief time at the conclusion of the end times (Rev. 17:12). Internal discord will turn the beast and these ten confederate kings against the city, and they will burn it, God having put into their hearts to fulfill His will (Rev. 17:16, 17). Then the beast and these kings will make war with the Lord Himself (Rev. 17:14) (See ARMAGEDDON).

The description of this future city has raised some questions as to its identity. Two leading interpretations have been given:

1. "Mystery Babylon" describes symbolically a great centralized system of wickedness in the end time.

2. "Mystery Babylon" refers to the old literal city of Babylon on the Euphrates, which will be restored as the

world's leading city of commerce and iniquity in the end time.

Those who affirm the latter view claim that certain prophecies concerning ancient Babylon have never been literally fulfilled, and hence, Babylon must be restored to future glory and world prestige in order to fulfill them.

### Prophecies Concerning Babylon

1. *Isaiah 13:19, 20*

   a. Babylon will be as when God overthrew Sodom and Gomorrah.
   b. It will never be inhabited.
   c. Neither will the Arabian pitch tent there.
   d. Neither will the shepherds make their fold there.

2. *Jeremiah 50:3, 8, 39, 40.*

   a. None will dwell in Babylon; it will not be inhabited; it will be wholly desolate.
   b. The Jews in captivity were exhorted to remove out of the midst of Babylon.
   c. It will not be inhabited forever.
   d. Neither will it be dwelt in from generation to generation.

3. *Jeremiah 51:6, 26, 43, 45.*

   a. The Jews were urged to flee out of the midst of Babylon before its destruction and deliver themselves: ". . . be not cut off in her iniquity; for this is the time of the Lord's vengeance."
   b. None would take of Babylon a stone for building purposes; it would be desolate forever.
   c. Babylon would become desolate heaps, a dwelling place for "dragons," an astonishment without an inhabitant.

d. The Lord spoke to cut off Babylon that none would remain in it, neither man nor beast, but it would become desolate forever.

4. *Jeremiah 25:17-26, 30-33.*

Babylon (Sheshach, verse 26) will drink of the cup of the Lord's wrath *last* of all the powers of the earth. Jewish and other interpreters agree that Sheshach has reference to Babylon (Henry C. Thiessen; R. A. Torrey; *Cambridge Bible*).

### Arguments for the Restoration of a Literal Babylon

Those who interpret these prophecies as not having been fulfilled in the past history of Babylon support their views as follows:

1. Babylon was not overthrown as suddenly and completely as were the cities of Sodom and Gomorrah, never to be found. The sites of Sodom and Gomorrah have not been located by archaeologists, but there is no doubt as to the location of ancient Babylon. At present there are several small, but growing, cities located on the site of Babylon, one of which retains the ancient name Babylon.

2. The prophecies of Jeremiah 51:11 were fulfilled in a measure in the capture of ancient Babylon by the Medes, but the destruction at that time did not result in any such utter destruction as described in Revelation 18.

3. When Babylon was captured in 538 B.C. by Cyrus the Great, Medo-Persian monarch, the city was left intact. Evidently the Israelites did not flee the city at that time as urged by the prophecies. Daniel, one of their prophets, along with most of Daniel's people remained and was captured by the Medes. This exhortation must refer, therefore, to the restored Babylon of the end times, for the exhortation is repeated in Revelation 18:4: "Come out of her, my people, that ye be not partakers of her sins, and that ye receive not of her plagues."

4. The city *gradually* disintegrated through the succeeding centuries. There never was sudden destruction as that which overtook Sodom and Gomorrah. In 500 B.C., Darius Hystaspis punished the Babylonians by throwing down the walls and gates because of an insurrection to gain emancipation from Persian bondage. Under Seleucas Nicator (died 280 B.C.) the city began to sink more rapidly when he built Seleucia on the Tigris from the ruins of Babylon and drew many inhabitants from Babylon. Peter the Apostle is believed to have written his epistles from Babylon in A.D. 64 (1 Peter 5:13). Jerome (fourth century) wrote that he had heard that the site of Babylon had been converted into a hunting ground for the recreation of Persian monarchs and that to preserve the game the walls had been repaired. Strabo (ninth century) said that in his time the place lay in ruins. There was a very small village on the site in 1100, however, and the name was changed from Babylon to Hillah. In 1888 the population was about 10,000, which grew to about 30,000 in 1936. (*Cyclopedia of Biblical, Theological and Ecclesiastical Literature; Encyclopedia Britannica,* fourteenth edition; *International Bible Encyclopedia*).

5. Today the cities on the site of ancient Babylon have a large Arab population, and their principal occupation is the shepherding of flocks.

6. Babylon's destruction as the fall of Sodom and Gomorrah is identified as occurring "in the day of the Lord," a time when "the stars of heaven and the constellations thereof shall not give their light; the sun shall be darkened in his going forth, and the moon shall not cause her light to shine" (Isa. 13:6, 10). Such events are described in the New Testament as to occur at the end of the tribulation period of end time (Matt. 6:12-17).

7. Israel was not given the "rest from sorrow, and from fear" which was promised as following the destruction of Babylon (Isa. 14:3, 4).

8. The bricks and stones from ancient Babylon have been used for building purposes, contrary to the prophecy of Jeremiah 51:26. Archaeologists have discovered bricks bearing the old Babylonian stamp in several other cities. The Greeks built Seleucia; the Parthians built Ctesiphon; the Persians built al Maiden; and the Caliphs built Kufa from the ruins of Babylon. Houses in Baghdad are also said to contain bricks bearing the old Babylonian stamp.

9. Babylon shall drink of the cup of the Lord's wrath *last* of all the kingdoms of the earth (Jer. 25:17-26).

10. Babylon is to be destroyed in one hour's time: "For in one hour so great riches is come to naught. . . . Alas, alas, that great city, wherein were made rich all that had ships in the sea by reason of her costliness, for in one hour is she made desolate" (Rev. 18:10, 17, 19). This has never yet been literally fulfilled.

11. Zechariah prophesies of the return of wickedness and commerce to Babylon (Zech. 5:5-11). But this prophecy was given to Zechariah *after* the fall of Babylon as a great kingdom in Old Testament history. His prophecy pictures two women carrying the ephah to the land of Shinar (Babylon) "to build it a base." Therefore, there must be a future restoration of the anicent city.

12. If Babylon is not a future literal city, it seems strange that the Holy Spirit would reveal its existence at the close of the tribulation judgments, together with such a detailed list of merchandise marketed in the city (Rev. 17 and 18): "The merchandise of gold, and silver, and precious stones, and of pearls, and fine linen, and purple, and silk, and scarlet, and all thyine wood, and all manner vessels of ivory, and all manner vessels of most precious wood, and of brass, and iron, and marble, and cinnamon, and odours, and ointments, and frankincense, and wine, and oil, and fine flour, and wheat, and beasts, and sheep, and horses, and chariots, and slaves, and souls of men" (Rev. 18:12, 13).

13. The present interest of the nations in the Near East makes the rebuilding of Babylon seem very likely. The area contains some of the richest oil fields of the world (See the following map). The Persian Gulf, for instance, supplied twenty-eight percent of all oil used in the world in 1970. Its lands contain sixty-two percent of all the world's oil reserves. The oil from this area alone supplies one half of Western Europe's oil and from ninety to ninety-five percent of Japan's needs. United States has seventy percent of the oil concessions. Russia spent two hundred million dollars on the development of the North Rumeila oil field near Kuwait in Iraq, which Premier Kosygin in person officially opened in April, 1972. In the event of a confrontation in the Middle East, this oil could be at the mercy of the dominant power.

According to the *Encyclopedia Americana,* a 26 million dollar plan is under study to excavate and restore ancient Babylon, including a new Tower of Babel and possibly the Hanging Gardens as tourist attractions.

### Arguments Against the Restoration of Literal Babylon

Those who affirm the view that literal Babylon will not be restored in the end time interpret "Mystery Babylon" (Rev. 17 and 18) as a figurative description of a great centralized system of wickedness rather than as a literal city. They support their view as follows:

1. The prophecies of Isaiah and Jeremiah were directed against the literal Babylon *of their day,* whose destruction they foretold. This is evident from the following:

   a. Babylon's ancient gods are named: Bel, Merodach (Jer. 50:2; 51:44).

   b. Specific geographical place of the ancient time are named: Lebanon (Isa. 14:8); Zion (Jer. 50:5); Assyria (Jer. 50:17); Carmel, Bashan, Ephraim, Gilead (Jer. 50:19); Jordan (Jer. 50:44); Judah (Jer. 51:5); Ararat, Minni, Ashchenaz (Jer. 51:27); Euphrates (Jer. 51:63).

c. Individuals and nations of that time are mentioned: King of the Medes (Isa. 13:17; Jer. 51:11, 28); Chaldeans (Isa. 13:19; Jer. 50:1, 8, 35, 45; 51:4); Jacob, Israel, Judah (Isa. 14:1, 2; Jer. 50:4, 33; 51:5); King of Babylon, Nebuchadnezzar (Isa. 14:4; Jer. 50:17, 43; 51:34); King of Assyria (Jer. 50:17); Seraiah the son of Neriah, the son of Maaseiah (Jer. 51:59); Zedekiah the King of Judah (Jer. 51:59).

d. Definite time references are given: Assyrian captivity is past (50:17, 18); these prophecies were given in the fourth year of the reign of Zedekiah (Jer. 51:59).

e. The name of the enemy who would destroy Babylon is prophesied: great nations from the north, the Medes, accompanied by the King of the Medes (Isa. 13:17; Jer. 50:3, 9, 41; 51:11).

2. The literal features of Babylon's destruction contained in these prophecies were fulfilled at the fall of Babylon to Medo-Persia in 538 B.C.

3. Any symbolical statements, such as Babylon's destruction being as when God overthrew Sodom and Gomorrah, never to be inhabited from generation to generation, is prophetic imagery of the destruction of Babylon in 538 B.C.

4. Zechariah's prophecy (Zech. 5:5-11) is symbolic of the cleansing of Israel and Palestine from the wickedness learned in the Babylonian captivity. Evil commercialism is to be sent back to the "land of Shinar," i.e. Babylon.

5. The city in Revelation 17 and 18 is called "Mystery Babylon." This city exercises dominion over "the kings of the earth"; "all nations"; "peoples and multitudes and nations and tongues." The fact that the word "Mystery" describes Babylon suggests not a literal city but a symbolic one, i.e., some power or system of the future.

## Bibliography

Evans, W. Glyn. "Will Babylon Be Restored?" *Our Hope,* 107:335-42
     (July, 1950); 107:481-87 (October, 1950).
Fortune, A. W. "Babylon," *International Standard Encyclopedia.* Grand
     Rapids, Michigan: William B. Eerdmans Publishing Company,
     1915.
Herrstrom, W. D. *The Next Gold Rush.* Akron, Ohio: Bible Blue Book
     Publishers, 1934.
"Hillah," *Encyclopedia Brittanica,* fourteenth edition; and *New Interna-
     tional Encyclopedia,* second edition.
McClintock, John and James Strong. "Babylon," *Cyclopedia of Biblical,
     Theological and Ecclesiastical Literature.* New York: Harper and
     Brothers, 1891.
Mackenzie, Herbert. "The Destruction of Babylon," *Bibliotheca Sacra,* 92:
     226-32 (April, 1935); 92:339-53 (July, 1935).
Newton, B. J. *Babylon: Its Future History and Doom.* London: Houlston
     and Sons, 1890.
Pember, G. H. *Antichrist, Babylon and the Coming Kingdom.* London:
     Hodder and Stoughton, no date.

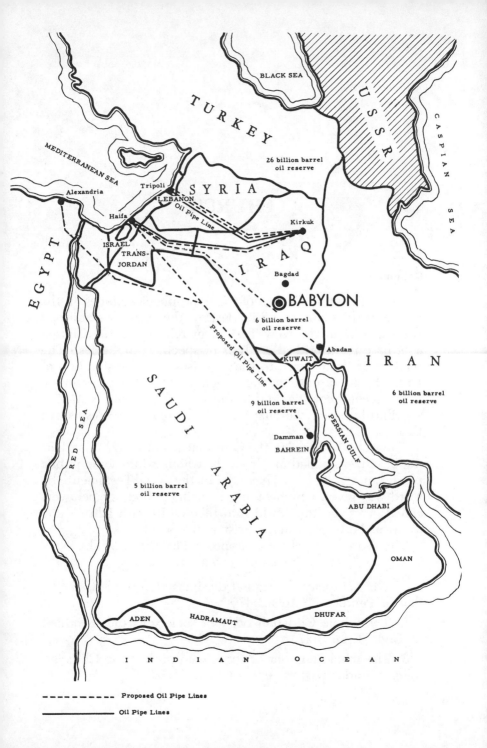

# CHURCH

## Definition

Since the interpretation of many prophecies hinges on the nature of the Church and its destiny, this chapter studies all the passages in the New Testament relating to the Church as a base for a critical analysis of specific prophecies. The relation of the Church to the promises of the restoration of Israel, to the rapture, to the millennium, to the resurrection, to the second coming, and to the great tribulation is studied specifically under the chapters which treat these respective themes.

The word "church" in the Greek means properly "a gathering of citizens called out from their homes into some public place: an assembly" (Thayer). In the New Testament the word was given new meaning as being a body of believers called out from the world into fellowship with Christ; one mystical body of which Christ is the head.

The word "church(es)" appears 115 times in the New Testament. It is the name given to:

1. The company of original disciples at Jerusalem on the day of Pentecost (Acts 2:47).

2. The whole Christian body or society as the sanctified of God (Eph. 5:27).

3. The whole number of those who profess the Christian religion under pastors, etc. (1 Cor. 12:18).

4. Particular societies of Christians in particular cities or provinces, i.e. the church in Jerusalem (Acts 8:1).

5. Particular assemblies of these societies and the places in which they met, e.g. "Greet the church that is in thy house," etc. (Rom. 16:5; 1 Cor. 11:18; 14:19, 28). (Adapted from McClintock and Strong)

## Names and Descriptions of the Church

1. My church (Matt. 16:18).
2. A spiritual house (1 Peter 2:5).
3. A holy priesthood (1 Peter 2:5).
4. The temple of God; a holy temple (Eph. 2:21; 1 Cor. 3:17; 6:19).
5. The body of Christ (1 Cor. 12:27; Eph. 4:4; Col. 1:24).
6. The bride of Christ (Eph. 5:27, 31, 32; Rev. 21:9).
7. The fullness of Christ (Eph. 1:23).
8. A glorious church (Eph. 5:27).
9. The church of the living God (1 Tim. 3:15).
10. The pillar and ground of the truth (1 Tim. 3:15).
11. The church of the firstborn (Heb. 12:23).
12. The church of God (1 Cor. 10:32; 15:9; Gal. 1:13).
13. Churches of the saints (1 Cor. 14:33).
14. The habitation of God (Eph. 2:22).

## Its Relationship to Christ

1. Christ is the head of His mystic body, the church (Col. 1:18; Eph. 1:22).
2. Christ died for the church; He is the Savior of the body (Acts 20:28; Eph. 5:23-25).
3. The church is cleansed and sanctified by Him (1 Cor. 6:11; Eph. 5:26, 27).
4. The church is loved, nourished and cherished by Him (Eph. 5:25, 29).
5. The church is subject to Him (Eph. 5:24).

6. The church was chosen in Him before the foundation of the world (Eph. 1:4).
7. The relationship of Christ to the church is called a great mystery (Eph. 5:32).
8. Christ is the foundation stone of the church (1 Cor. 3:11; Eph. 2:20; 1 Peter 2:6).

## Its Membership

1. The church is represented in the New Testament as the body of believers, those saved by His blood (Acts 2:47; Eph. 5:25).
2. Repentance, baptism, and faith in Christ are required of all its members (Matt. 16:16-18; Acts 2:38-41).

## Its Organization

1. Founded on Peter's confession: "Thou art the Christ, the Son of the living God" (Matt. 16:18).
2. The apostles and prophets, the foundation; Christ, the chief cornerstone; members, the building, fitly framed together into a holy temple (Eph. 2:20, 21).
3. One body; many assemblies constitute the membership of the one body (1 Cor. 12:12).
4. Indwelt by the Holy Spirit (John 14:17; Acts 2:4).
5. All members baptized into one body by the Spirit (1 Cor. 12:13).
6. The ministry, for the edifying of the church and the perfecting of the saints, consists of apostles, prophets, evangelists, pastors and teachers (Eph. 4:11, 12).
7. Bishops, deacons, elders, for the care and service of local churches (Acts 6:2-6; 14:23; 1 Tim. 3).

## Its Ordinances

1. Baptism (Matt. 29:19, 20; Mark 16:16; Acts 2:38, 41).
2. The Lord's Supper (Acts 2:42, 46; 20:7; 1 Cor. 11: 20-34).

## Its Calling and Destiny

1. To heavenly places (Col. 3:1, 2).
2. To holiness (Eph. 1:4; 2:21; 5:27).
3. To praise and glorify Him (Eph. 1:6; 3:21).
4. To a perfect man, to the measure of the stature of Christ (Eph. 4:13).
5. To preach the Gospel to the uttermost parts of the earth (Acts 1:8; Eph. 3:8).
6. Finally, to be raptured at Christ's coming in the clouds to be forever with Him, when its eternal purpose and destiny will be realized fully (1 Thess. 4:16, 17; Rev. 14:15, 16).

## Bibliography

Allis, Oswald T. *Prophecy and the Church.* Philadelphia: Presbyterian and Reformed, 1945.

Scofield, C. I. "The Return of Christ in Relation to the Church," *Bibliotheca Sacra,* 109:77-87 (January, 1952).

Wale, Burlington B. *The Closing Days of Christendom.* London, Partridge, no date.

Walvoord, John F. "Is the Church the Israel of God," *Bibliotheca Sacra,* 101:403-16 (October, 1944).

————— "Premillennialism and the Church," *Bibliotheca Sacra,* 110: 289-98 (October, 1953); 111:1-10 (January, 1954); 111:97-104 (April, 1954).

# DANIEL'S SEVENTY WEEKS

## Definition

The seventy weeks of Daniel, or the "seventy-sevens" as literally stated in the Hebrew text, refer to the time of Jerusalem's desolation under Gentile rule (Dan. 9:2, 12, 16). In answer to Daniel's prayer for enlightenment regarding the duration of the Babylonian Captivity, God revealed to Daniel that the seventy years of the Babylonian Captivity as prophesied by Jeremiah would be extended to "seventy-sevens." These "seventy-sevens" of years are often referred to as the "Times of the Gentiles" that are determined upon Daniel's people.

## Biblical Reference

The reference to the seventy weeks appears only in Daniel 9:24-27:

> Seventy weeks are determined upon thy people and upon thy holy city, to finish the transgression, and to make an end of sins, and to make reconciliation for iniquity, and to bring in everlasting righteousness, and to seal up the vision and prophecy, and to anoint the most Holy. Know therefore and understand, that from the going forth of the commandment to restore and to build Jerusalem unto the Messiah the Prince shall be seven weeks, and threescore and two weeks: the street shall be built again, and the wall, even in troublous times. And after threescore and two weeks shall Messiah be cut off, but not for himself: and

the people of the prince that shall come shall destroy the
city and the sanctuary; and the end thereof shall be with
a flood, and unto the end of the war desolations are determined. And he shall confirm the covenant with many for
one week: and in the midst of the week he shall cause
the sacrifice and the oblation to cease, and for the over-
spreading of abominations he shall make it desolate, even
until the consummation, and that determined shall be
poured upon the desolate.

### The Beginning of the Seventy Weeks

The beginning of these "seventy-sevens" was revealed to
Daniel as being the time of the command or decree to
rebuild and to restore the city of Jerusalem (Dan. 9:25; cf.
Neh. 2:1-8). This decree was given in the first of the month
Nisan in the twentieth year of the reign of Artaxerxes, 445
B.C. (Neh. 2:1). Other decrees mentioned in the book of
Ezra (1:1, 2; 4:1-5, 11-24; 6:1-5, 14, 15; 7:11, 20, 27) refer
to the rebuilding of the temple and not of the city.

The accession of Artaxerxes to the throne took place in
465 B.C. That makes his twentieth year 445 B.C. For the
calculation of the first of Nisan (Neh. 2:1) as March 14,
445 B.C., see Sir Robert Anderson's *The Coming Prince*, p.
124. Sir Robert Anderson obtained this date from the Royal
Astronomer at Greenwich, England.

### The Division of the Seventy-Sevens

The seventy-sevens are divided into three sections: seven,
sixty-two, and one. The first section of seven sevens and the
second section of sixty-two sevens end with Messiah's being cut off, i.e. at the crucifixion of Chirst. The third and
last section consisting of only one seven is distinguished
by a covenant that is confirmed by the "prince that shall
come" with the Israelites. The prince breaks the covenant
in the middle of the last seven. At the conclusion of the
entire seventy-sevens the vision and the prophecy will be
completely fulfilled, and "everlasting righteousness" will be
brought in.

### The End of the Sixty-Ninth Seven

The end of the sixty-ninth seven marks the cutting off of the Messiah. Based on Luke 3:1, Sir Robert Anderson calculates this date as April 6, A.D. 32. The public ministry of Christ began in the fifteenth year of Tiberias Caesar, who began the first year of his reign in A.D. 14, according to the date given in the *Westminster Atlas*.

From 445 B.C. to A.D. 32 is 476 years, counting 1 B.C. and A.D. 1 as one year. These 476 years mark the duration of the sixty-nine weeks beginning with the decree of Artaxerxes in 445 B.C. to rebuild Jerusalem up to the time when Messiah is cut off in A.D. 32. From this it becomes evident that each seven is equal to one seven-year period.

To demonstrate the accuracy of these figures, attention has been directed to the fact that biblical years are made up of 360 days per year instead of 365. This can be seen in the duration of the flood mentioned as being five months in Genesis 7:11 and 8:4 while the same period is spoken of as being 150 days in Genesis 7:24 and 8:3. Also in the book of Revelation 42 months are identified with 1260 days and with "a time, and times, and half a time," one and a half years (Rev. 13:4-7; 12:6, 13, 14).

### The Seventieth Week

Because the seventieth week of Daniel is mentioned as occurring after the cutting off of Messiah, two different views as to its place in history have arisen:

1. The seventieth week follows *immediately* after the sixty-ninth. In that case the seventieth week would end seven years later in the early part of the history recorded in the book of Acts. This does not seem likely since during this time there was no "end of transgressions" on the part of Daniel's people, as prophesied, but rather an increase. And "everlasting righteousness" obviously has not been brought in even yet. Amillenarians, however, interpret the

"everlasting righteousness" as spiritually realized at the first coming of Christ.

2. The seventieth week is still *future*. This seems clear from the mention of the abomination of desolation (Dan. 9:27) which Christ identified with the end time and with His second coming (Matt. 24:15, 21, 29, 30). This interpretation leaves room for the destruction of the city of Jerusalem (Dan. 9:26), which did not take place until A.D. 70. Also the length of the "time of the end" or the second half of the seventieth week is in exact harmony with the time dimensions of a future tribulation period as described in the book of the Revelation (cf. Dan. 12:7 with Rev. 12:14 and 13:5).

The seventieth week will begin when the great world political leader of the end time will make a covenant with Daniel's people, Israel. The covenant may grant permission for a "daily sacrifice," as inferred from its mention when the covenant is prophesied as being broken in the middle of the week. The breaking of the covenant in the middle of the week and the erection of the abomination of desolation will mark the beginning of the time of the end, a time of great and unparalleled tribulation in world history just before the second coming of Christ. The close of the seventieth week will mark the introduction of the blessings mentioned in Daniel 9:24.

For the historical arrangement of the seventy weeks, see the accompanying diagram.

## Bibliography

Anderson, Robert. *The Coming Prince*. London: Hodder and Stoughton, 1909.

Ironside, H. A. *The Great Parenthesis*. Grand Rapids, Michigan: Zondervan Publishing House, 1943.

————. *Lectures on Daniel the Prophet*. New York: Loizeaux Brothers, no date.

Kelly, William. *Notes on Daniel*. New York: Loizeaux Brothers, no date.

Knowles, Louis E. "The Interpretation of the Seventy Weeks of Daniel in the Early Fathers," *Westminster Theological Journal*, 7:2 (May, 1945).

Leupold, H. C. *Exposition of Daniel.* Columbus, Ohio: Wartburg Press, 1949.

McClain, Alva J. *Daniel's Prophecy of the Seventy Weeks.* Grand Rapids, Michigan: Zondervan Publishing House, 1940.

Mauro, Philip. *The Seventy Weeks and the Great Tribulation.* Boston: Hamilton Brothers, 1923.

Stevens, W. C. *The Book of Daniel.* New York: Fleming H. Revell Company, 1918.

Tregelles, S. P. *Remarks on the Prophetic Visions of the Book of Daniel.* London: Samuel Bagster and Sons, 1883.

Walvoord, John F. "Is the Seventieth Week of Daniel Future?" *Bibliotheca Sacra,* 101:30-49 (January, 1944).

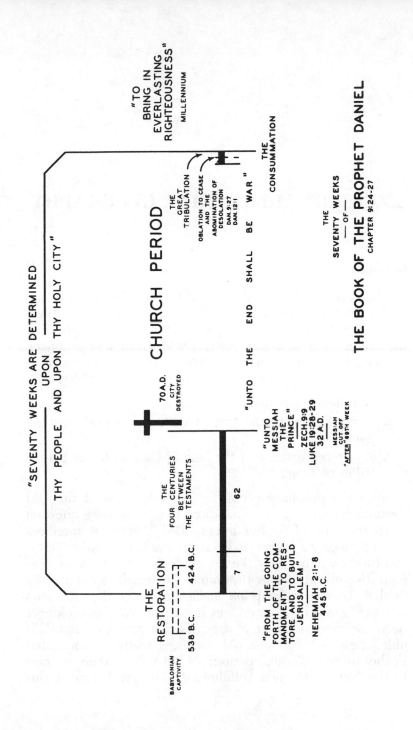

"SEVENTY WEEKS ARE DETERMINED
UPON
THY PEOPLE AND UPON THY HOLY CITY"

"TO BRING IN EVERLASTING RIGHTEOUSNESS"
MILLENNIUM

CHURCH PERIOD

THE GREAT TRIBULATION

OBLATION TO CEASE AND THE ABOMINATION OF DESOLATION
DAN. 9:27
DAN. 12:1

THE CONSUMMATION

"UNTO    THE    END    SHALL    BE    WAR"

70 A.D.
CITY DESTROYED

THE FOUR CENTURIES BETWEEN THE TESTAMENTS

"UNTO MESSIAH THE PRINCE"
ZECH. 9:9
LUKE 19:28-29
32 A.D.

MESSIAH CUT OFF
"AFTER" 69TH WEEK

62

7

THE RESTORATION

538 B.C.

424 B.C.

BABYLONIAN CAPTIVITY

"FROM THE GOING FORTH OF THE COMMANDMENT TO RESTORE AND TO BUILD JERUSALEM"
NEHEMIAH 2:1-8
445 B.C.

THE BOOK OF THE PROPHET DANIEL

THE
SEVENTY WEEKS
— OF —
CHAPTER 9:24-27

# EZEKIEL'S MILLENNIAL GEOGRAPHY

## Definition

Chapters 40 - 48 of the book of the prophet Ezekiel describe a future restoration and blessedness of Israel. Fourteen years after the fall of Jerusalem and the capture of the Israelites in 572 B.C., Ezekiel was given this prophecy concerning Israel's restoration from captivity. Three main features of the restoration promised in this prophecy are:

1. A restored sanctuary;
2. A restored sacrificial system with new service and organization;
3. A restored division of the land of Canaan to the twelve tribes of Israel.

Since the prophecy promises the restoration of the Old Testament sacrificial system, there has been some question as to the time of its fulfillment. Old Testament sacrifices and offerings no longer have any meaning in New Testament times. The New Testament refers to them as prefigurative object lessons to remind the Israelites continually of their coming redemption in Christ. Since the One who was prefigured in the sacrifices has come, there is no longer need for the old object lessons. Is this prophecy unfulfillable, then, or will these old sacrifices really be reinstated in the future millennial period? What will be their relation to the New Testament fulfillment? The resolution of this problem has taken three forms of interpretation: literal, figurative, and conditional. The main tenets of each position are listed as follows:

### For a Literal Fulfillment

1. Its chronological sequences. If Ezekiel is understood to be in chronological sequence, then the restoration of the temple and sacrifices happens *after* the restoration of Israel to Palestine. This could not refer to the temple of Zerubbabel which Israel built on its return from Babylon. Zerubbabel's temple was built on previous patterns of the Mosaic tabernacle and the temple of Solomon (Ezra 6:3; Ezek. 41: 12, 13; cf. 1 Maccabees 4:47, 60; Sirach 50:1ff.); Ezekiel's blueprint of the temple is not referred to in the measurements of the Restoration Temple of Zerubbabel.

2. Its definite commands. If these commands are not literal and definite, it becomes difficult to understand how God could expect their fulfillment.

3. Its detailed ordinances of worship.

4. Its mention of definite names of individuals and locations.

5. Its very minute measurement and architectural peculiarities. If these ordinances, names and measurements are not literal and definite, it becomes difficult to understand why Ezekiel was not given an interpretation of the symbolism as was usually the case (Ezek. 1:4-28; 4:1-17; 5:1-17; 17:1-21).

6. Its identity of the twelve tribes (Matt. 19:28) indicates a future time when those who had followed the Lord Jesus Christ in the regeneration would reign on twelve thrones judging the twelve tribes of Israel.

Those who hold to this literal realization of Ezekiel's prophecy assert the following:

1. The temple of Herod cannot be identified with the description given by Ezekiel.

2. Since no such temple as described by Ezekiel has existed up to the present, the fulfillment of this prophecy can only belong to some future period such as the millennium, or to the time of Israel's restoration to the land before the millennium.

3. The temple described in Ezekiel does not belong to the postmillennial eternal state, as seen by the following contrast between Ezekiel 40 - 48 and Revelation 21 and 22:

| Ezekiel 40 - 48 | Revelation 21, 22 |
| --- | --- |
| Ezekiel describes a temple. | John says, "I saw no temple therein." |
| Ezekiel's land is bounded by the sea. | John says, ". . . and there was no more sea." |
| Ezekiel speaks of the land of Israel. | John speaks of a new heaven and a new earth. |
| Ezekiel describes the city as being in the land of Canaan. | John sees the holy city coming down out of heaven. |
| Ezekiel sees the glory as dwelling in the temple. | John sees the glory lighting the whole city. |
| The temple in Ezekiel is only a little less than one mile square. | The city, New Jerusalem, in the Revelation is somewhat more than 1300 miles square. |

4. This restored sacrificial system will become in the future the means of Israel's expressing national worship and devotion as also foretold by other prophets. The worship may well be commemorative in nature (Isa. 2:3, 4; 66:22, 23; Zech. 14:16-21). The complete Levitical system will not be reinstated. The only feasts mentioned in Ezekiel 40 - 48 as being reinstated are the Feasts of the Passover and of the Tabernacles, which even in Old Testament times were commemorative.

5. This millennial restoration will be characterized by a new division of the land, by a new name for Jerusalem, by the portion of the prince, and by "living waters."

## For a Figurative Fulfillment

Amillennarians, whose principle of interpretation of Scriptures is the spiritualization of the text, offer the following explanations:

1. The restoration figuratively prefigures the gracious presence of the Lord in His Church, which will manifest itself when He shall come again. (Carl Friedrich Keil)

2. The promises of a restored temple refer primarily to the rebuilt temple of restoration days, with some elements referring to the new heaven and the new earth. (Martin J. Wyngaarden)

3. The restoration prophecy symbolizes the manifestation of the Kingdom of God on earth in government, in the Church, and in civilization as God meant them to be. (Floyd Hamilton, Edmund Clowney)

A comparison of these amillennial explanations with the text of Ezekiel's prophecy obviously presents more and greater difficulties than those which arise from the literal interpretation of the premillennarians.

## For a Conditional Fulfillment

Ezekiel's prophecy is conditioned upon Israel's repentance (Ezek. 43:9-11). Israel did not repent; hence, they have become unworthy of such a reconstruction, and the prophecy is rendered invalid. This view is set forth by George Peters (Proposition 172, *The Theocratic Kingdom*, vol. 3). Peters makes the following assertions:

1. The prince cannot be Christ, whose coming would "restore" Israel, since:

   a. He is exhorted not to do wrong (Ezek. 45:16-18).

   b. He has a family; thus, he is only a mortal man (Ezek. 46:16).

   c. He prepares a sin offering for himself (Ezek. 45:22).

   d. Priests prepare the burnt offering and peace offering for the prince (Ezek. 42:2).

   e. The prince is given to sinful oppression (Ezek. 45:9-11).

2. If the prince is a mortal who rules over the Jewish nations in the future millennial restoration under or subject to Christ, the following difficulties arise:

   a. Then this is a lengthy millennial description without Christ being introduced at all, which is unlikely.

   b. A prince would be reigning on David's throne, whereas Christ is the real heir to the throne of David.

   c. A mortal man would be ruling over the twelve tribes of Israel that were assigned by Christ to the twelve apostles under His headship.

   d. The millennial rulership would be vested in a person liable to sin.

3. Passages which speak of worship and sacrifice in the prophecy are not to be interpreted as a return to the Old Testament Mosaic ritual. They are to be understood, instead, under the extended priesthood of the New Testament where "sacrifice" is used of Christian worship, conduct, acts of benevolence, and love (Rom. 12:1; 15:16; Phil. 2:17; 4:18; 1 Peter 2:5, 9; Heb. 13:15).

The word "temple," too, must not be understood literally. It involves the union of the believer with Christ (1 Cor. 3:16; 2 Cor. 6:16; Rev. 3:12; 7:15; 21:22).

For the geography of the restored division of the land of Canaan to the twelve tribes, see the accompanying map.

## Bibliography

Bezzant, R., and R. P. Pridham. *The Promise of Ezekiel's City.* Norwich, England: Simpkins, 1952.

Chafer, Rollin Thomas. "The Boundaries of Greater Canaan," *Bibliotheca Sacra,* 95:231-36 (April, 1938).

Clowney, Edmund P. "The Final Temple," *Prophecy in the Making,* ed. Carl F. H. Henry. Wheaton, Illinois: Creation House, 1971.

Davidson, A. B. *The Book of Ezekiel.* Cambridge, 1896.

DeHaan, M. R. *The Jew and Palestine in Prophecy.* Grand Rapids, Michigan: Zondervan Publishing House, 1950.

Feinberg, Charles Lee. "The Rebuilding of the Temple," *Prophecy in the Making,* ed. Carl F. H. Henry. Wheaton, Illinois: Creation House, 1971.

Fisch, S. *Ezekiel.* London: Soncino Series, 1950.

Gaebelein, Arno C. *The Prophet Ezekiel.* New York: Our Hope, 1918.

Ironside, H. A. *Expository Notes on Ezekiel the Prophet.* New York: Loizeaux Brothers, 1949.

Keil, Carl Friedrich. *Prophecies of Ezekiel.* Edinburg: T. and T. Clark, no date.

Kelly, William. *Notes on Ezekiel.* London: G. Morrish, no date.

Mitchell, John L. "The Question of Millennial Sacrifices," *Bibliotheca Sacra,* 110:248-67 (July, 1953); 110:342-45 (October, 1953).

Newberry, Thomas. *The Temple of Solomon and Ezekiel.* Glasgow: Pickering and Inglis, no date.

Payne, James. *The Millennial Temple of Ezekiel's Prophecy.* London, 1947.

Richardson, Stanton. *The Relation of the Church and Israel to the Millennium.* Unpublished Thesis. Wheaton, Illinois: Wheaton College, 1946.

Unger, Merrill F. "Ezekiel's Vision of Israel's Restoration," *Bibliotheca Sacra,* 106:312-24 (July, 1949); 106:432-45 (October, 1949); 107:51-70 (January, 1950).

————— "The Temple Vision of Ezekiel," *Bibliotheca Sacra,* 105:418-32; (October, 1948); 106:48-64 (January, 1949); 106:169-77 (April, 1949).

White, F. H. *The Land, the City, and the Temple of Israel in the Millennium: Ezekiel 40-48.* London: Partridge, no date.

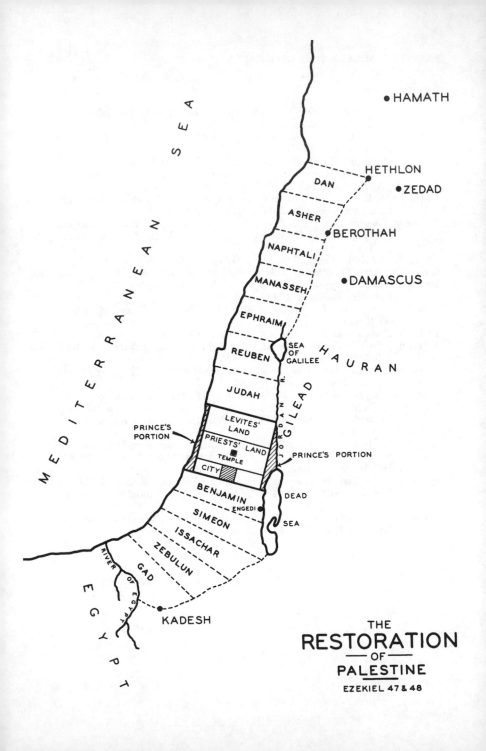

THE
RESTORATION
—OF—
PALESTINE
EZEKIEL 47 & 48

# GOG AND MAGOG

## Definition

God and Magog refer to the lands and the people that will invade the land of Israel in future times.

## Biblical References

The names Gog, Magog, and Hamon-Gog appear in the Bible in the following places:

GOG:     (1 Chron. 5:4; Ezek. 38:2, 3, 14, 15, 18; 39:1, 11; Rev. 20:8).

MAGOG:   (Gen. 10:2; 1 Chron. 1:5; Ezek. 38:2; 39:6; Rev. 20:8).

HAMON-GOG: (Ezek. 39:11, 15).

These passages present the following information concerning Gog, Magog, and Hamon-Gog:

1. *Reason for Gog's Invasion*
   Gog will invade Israel to gain the possession of the land (Ezek. 38:12, 13).

2. *Time of Gog's Invasion*
   The time of Gog's invasion is referred to as follows:
   a. "After many days, in the after years" (Ezek. 38:8).
   b. "In the latter days" (Ezek. 38:16).
   c. "At the time of Israel's regathering" (Ezek. 38:8, 11, 12, 13; 39:27, 28).
   d. After the millennial reign of Christ (Rev. 20:7, 8).

Some Bible teachers identify the invasion of Gog and Magog in Ezekiel with the invasion of Gog and Magog in the book of Revelation, chapter 20. Others place the invasion prophesied by Ezekiel just before the millennium or at the close of the tribulation period, making the battle of Armageddon and the invasion of Gog and Magog synonymous. In this future invasion of Israel the confederates with Gog will be Persia (Iran), Ethiopia, Libya, Gomer, and Togarmah. The first three are known as nations today. The identity of Gomer and Togarmah is somewhat obscure.

Still other Bible teachers state that there are two invasions of Israel by Gog and Magog. The first invasion occurs before the millennium, and the second occurs after the millennium. Those holding this view have suggested that the second invasion may be called an invasion of "Gog and Magog," as a poetic allusion to the former Gog and Magog. That is, the future invading nations wish to declare their enmity against Israel to be as ferocious as that which characterized Israel's ancient enemies.

However the time of Gog's invasion of Israel is determined, the following comparison of Ezekiel 38, 39 and Revelation 20 should prove helpful:

| Gog in Ezekiel | Gog in Revelation |
| --- | --- |
| Both are destroyed by fire. (Ezek. 38:22) | (Rev. 20:9) |
| God brings Gog forth. (Ezek. 38:4) | Satan brings Gog forth. (Rev. 20:7, 8) |
| Gog comes from the North. (Ezek. 38:6) | Gog comes from the four corners of the earth. (Rev. 20:8) |
| Gog is a "multitude." (Ezek. 39:11) | Gog is as the sand of the sea. (Rev. 20:8) |
| Gog is set forth as the final enemy against Israel. (Ezek. 38:8, 14-16) | (Rev. 20:7, 8) |

3. *Final Destruction of Gog*

Gog is described in Ezekiel as an unmanageable beast compelled to follow a leader. Gog will be destroyed by the judgment of God as follows:

1. By mutiny in the ranks of Gog's army (Ezek. 38:21);
2. By pestilence (Ezek. 38:22);
3. By supernatural rain and hail of fire and brimstone (Ezek. 38:22).

The result of this destruction will be: (a) that God is sanctified (Ezek. 38:16); and (b) that the prophecy might be proved true (Ezek. 38:17; 39:23, 28).

In Ezekiel 38:2, 3 an interesting difference between the texts of the Authorized and Revised Versions appears. In the Authorized Version the expression "chief prince of Meshech and Tubal" appears, whereas in the Revised Version the phrase, "prince of Rosh, Meshech and Tubal" appears. These two translations for the same passage differ because the Hebrew word translated "chief" (A.V.) is "Rosh," which means "head" or "chief." "Rosh," however, has been taken as a proper name in the Revised Version and is, therefore, translated "prince of Rosh, Meshech and Tubal," indicating people or territory. In the Authorized Version the word "Rosh" is translated as an adjective describing "the prince of Meshech and Tubal." But the question remains: Is Rosh a proper name of a people of whom Gog is the prince, or is Rosh an adjective modifying prince, as "chief prince"?

The view of the Authorized Version, "chief prince," was held also by Ewald, Aquila, and Jerome, after the analogy of 1 Chronicles 27:5 where Rosh is translated "chief priest." The view of the Revised Version was held by Keil and Delitzsch, following the Septuagint, and hence, the passage refers to three distinct people: Rosh, Meshech and Tubal. Keil claims that Byzantine and Arabic writers mention a people called Rus living in the country of Taurus, who were counted among the Scythian tribes.

### Identity of Gog

1. The first appearance of the name Gog in Scripture is the mention of a Reubenite (1 Chron. 5:4), but nothing more is known about him.

2. In Ezekiel, Gog appears as the name of the king or prince of Magog (38ff), who is described also as prince of Rosh, Meshech and Tubal. From the far distant northern lands he will invade Palestine with a confederacy of nations in the last days. Speculation as to who will be the invaders of the end time are:

   a. The northern (European) powers, headed up by Russia, as indicated by the reference to Meshech and Tubal, i.e. Moscow and Tobolsk. (Scofield)

   b. The great Scythian people. Gog is probably a name formed by Ezekiel as the name of the prince who is from Magog, the home of the Scythians. Rosh, Meshech and Tubal are people who lived in the neighborhood of Magog. (Keil)

   c. An Assyrian, Gâgu, chief of a mountain tribe north of Assyria. (Delitzsch)

   d. "Gog is a Hebrew obstruction of Goga that survived long after the Gasga folk passed into oblivion. . . . Gasga is mentioned with Haniqalbat and Ugarit as a barbarian country to the north. . . . In the writer's opinion, Gaga is a slight corruption of Gasga, a name applied in the Boghaz-kai tablets to a wild mountainous district north of Melitene on the confines of Armenia and Cappadocia" (W. F. Albright, *Journal of Biblical Literature*, 43:381, 383) (1942).

3. The mention of Gog in Revelation 20 seems to refer to the name of a region rather than to an individual.

### Identity of Magog

The land of Gog is located in the Bible as being in the "uttermost parts of the north" (Ezek. 38:6, 15; 39:2). From the historical research recorded below, it seems that Gog and Magog refer to a barbarian people and land directly north of the land of Israel just below the Black Sea (see map).

The name Magog first appears in Scriptures as a son of Japheth (Gen. 10:2) and then refers later to the great and powerful people descended from Japheth as well as the region where they lived, in the extreme recesses of the north. A few of the views of their identification are:

1. Magog really means "the land of Gog," the mountainous region between Cappadocia and Media. Josephus the Jewish historian said that "Gomer founded those whom the Greeks now call Galatians. . . . Magog founded those that from him are called Magogites, who are by the Greek called Scythians . . . Mosheni were founded by Moshoch; now they are Cappadocians" (*Antiquities of the Jews,* 1:6, 1).

2. "Magog is a blend of Manda the regular Mesopotamian designation for northern barbarians and Gog the Hebrew equivalent" (W. F. Albright).

3. The region of Magog was what is known today as the Caucasus and its steppes. Rosh, Meshech and Tubal were Scythians, barbarous nomadic tribes who roamed around the Black and Caspian Seas. This territory north of Palestine is now in the hands of Russia. The prince of Rosh is the leader of the Russian empire. He also is in control of Meshech and Tubal, which are reproduced in the modern Moscow and Tobolsk. The man who will lead this confederacy of nations against Israel, then, is a Russian. Gomer has prophetic reference to Germany, to which the descendants of Gomer migrated (Arno Gaebelein).

### Identity of Hamon-Gog

"Hamon," from a Hebrew root meaning "to hum, growl, sigh, or moan," is used in the Bible for the noise of a multitude of people. As used by Ezekiel, then, the "multitude of Gog" would seem to express tumultuous confusion made by great numbers of people, and would refer to Gog's confederated allies.

### Identity of Gomer

The first mention of Gomer in the Scriptures was as the oldest son of Japheth (Gen. 10:2, 3). Most interpreters understand the "Gomer" of Ezekiel, however, to refer to the Germans, who are reputed to be the descendants of the Celts, who descended from Gomer, who were in turn the Cimmerii who lived in early times just north of the Black Sea in the Crimea. Historians claim that the Cimmerii abandoned this residence in a war with the Scythians and settled in western Asia Minor (800 - 700 B.C.) until their expulsion about fifty years later. After their expulsion their name disappears from history in its original form, and hence, is held to be identical with the Celtic race, the Cimbri of northern Europe, sometimes described by classicists as the Germans (Condensed from McClintock and Strong's *Encyclopedia*).

Gomer is allied with Gog of the land of Magog, chief prince of Meshech and Tubal, or prince of Rosh, Meshech, and Tubal.

### Identity of Togarmah

The first appearance of Togarmah in Scripture is as one of the three sons of Gomer (Gen. 10:3). Ezekiel mentioned the descendants of Togarmah as trading with the merchants of Tyre "in its fairs with horses, and horsemen, and mules" (Ezek. 27:14). The Jews understood them to be the Turks who descended from the Turkoman hordes, since the Septuagint and some Hebrew manuscripts render the word Togarma. Others have rather connected them with the Armenians since (1) Armenia was distinguished by the production of good horses according to one historian; and (2) Togarmah comes from the Sanskrit *toka*, "tribe," and Arma-, i.e. Armenia.

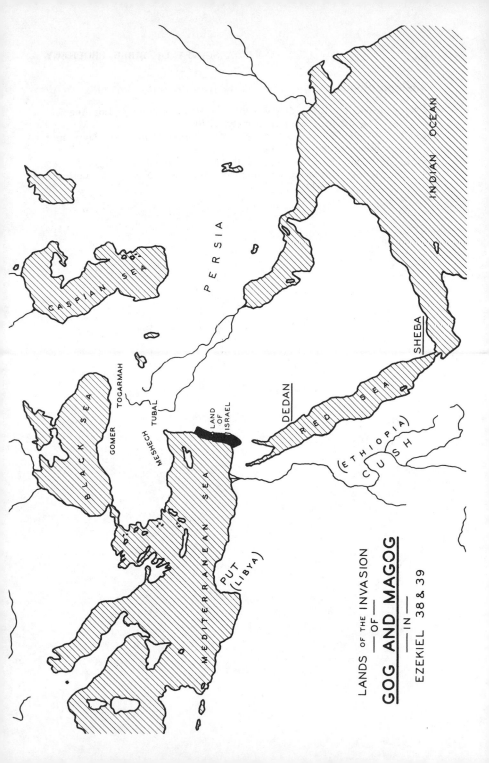

LANDS of the INVASION
— OF —
**GOG AND MAGOG**
— IN —
EZEKIEL 38 & 39

## Bibliography

Cooper, David L. *When Gog's Armies Meet the Almighty.* Los Angeles: The Biblical Research Society, 1940.

Lindberg, Milton B. *Gog All Agog "in the Latter Days."* Findlay, Ohio: Fundamental Truth Publishers, 1939.

Wale, Burlington B. "The Way of the Kings of the East," *Light for the World's Darkness,* ed. John W. Bradbury. New York: Loizeaux Brothers, 1944.

# JUDGMENTS

## Definition

Both the Old and the New Testaments teach that there will be a final future judgment for believers and unbelievers, for the Gentile nations as well as for Israel. Judgment is as certain as Christ's resurrection from the dead (Acts 17:31). The great event will take place at the end of this age when the Lord Jesus returns (1 Cor. 4:5; Matt. 25:31, 32; 2 Tim. 4:1; 2 Thess. 1:7-10; Phil. 3:18-21; Matt. 13:39, 49; John 12:48).

There are two great judgments, one preceding the millennium, "the first resurrection" (Rev. 20:4, 5), and one following the millennium, "the great white throne" judgment (Rev. 20:5, 11, 15).

A few of the great "judgment" passages in Scripture are:

> For he cometh, for he cometh to judge the earth: he shall judge the world with righteousness, and the people with his truth (Ps. 96:13).

> For God shall bring every work into judgment, with every secret thing, whether it be good, or whether it be evil (Eccl. 12:14).

> Because he hath appointed a day, in the which he will judge the world in righteousness by that man whom he hath ordained; whereof he hath given assurance unto all men, in that he hath raised him from the dead (Acts 17:31).

And as it is appointed unto men once to die, but after this the judgment (Heb. 9:27).

And I saw thrones, and they sat upon them, and judgment was given unto them: and I saw the souls of them that were beheaded for the witness of Jesus, and for the word of God and which had not worshipped the beast, neither his image, neither had received his mark upon their foreheads, or in their hands; and they lived and reigned with Christ a thousand years. But the rest of the dead lived not again until the thousand years were finished. This is the first resurrection. . . . And I saw a great white throne, and him that sat on it, from whose face the earth and the heaven fled away, and there was found no place for them. And I saw the dead, small and great, stand before God; and the books were opened: and another book was opened, which is the book of life: and the dead were judged out of those things which were written in the books, according to their works (Rev. 20:4, 5, 11, 12).

## THE JUDGE: The Lord Jesus Christ

For the Father judgeth no man, but hath committed all judgment unto the Son: that all men should honor the Son, even as they honor the Father. He that honoreth not the Son honoreth not the Father which hath sent him. . . . And hath given him authority to execute judgment also, because he is the Son of man (John 5:22, 23, 27).

And he commanded us to preach unto the people, and to testify that it is he which was ordained of God to be the Judge of quick and dead (Acts 10:42).

### Subjects of Judgment

### 1. *Believers*

Those who believe, both living and dead, will be judged before Christ's millennial reign (Rev. 20:4, 5) at "the first resurrection." If a comparison of Matthew 19:28 and 2 Corinthians 5:10 implies that the Apostles will be judged before the tribes of Israel over whom they will become judges, then by analogy believers in general will be judged before they become judges (Rev. 20:4; 1 Cor. 6:2, 3).

### 2. Unbelievers

The wicked dead will be judged at the "great white throne" judgment *after* the millennial reign (Rev. 20:5, 12).

### 3. Satan and the fallen angels

Satan will be judged both before and after the millennial reign. Before the millennium he is bound and cast into the bottomless pit for the duration. After the millennium he is released for a "little season." Then he will be judged and cast into the lake of fire (Rev. 20).

## Principles of Judgment

The Bible states generally that all shall be judged according to their works which are written in God's records (Rev. 20:12). The main principle of judgment, which determines eternal righteousness or damnation, rests on an individual's trust in God and His plan of salvation. The unbelieving nations seem to be judged by God's law written on their hearts (Rom. 2:12-16), and by their attitude of kindness or unkindness toward Israel, and toward New Testament believers, the "brethren" of their Judge (Gen. 12:3; Zech. 12:9; Matt. 25:40). Israel will be judged and purged on the way back to Palestine and at the Lord's return (Mal. 3:2-5). This judgment will decide the question as to the Israel that will enter the Kingdom age (Ezek. 20: 33-44; Rev. 12:6, 13-17; 7:1-8).

## The Sentence or Rewards of Judgment

1. Believers are all saved; some are rewarded (1 Cor. 3: 11-15). Crowns will be given at the judgment seat of Christ. For a list of the crowns, see the section on "Relation of the Millennium to the Second Coming" under PREMILLENNIALISM.

2. The wicked dead — those not found written in the book of life — will be cast into the lake of fire (Rev. 19:15).

3. Satan and the fallen angels, the beast and the false prophet, are cast into the lake of fire (Rev. 19:20; 20:10).

## Bibliography

English, E. Schuyler. "The Judgment of the Nations." *Our Hope*, 51: 561-65 (February, 1948).

————— "The Judgment Seat of Christ." *Our Hope*, 51:416-22 (December, 1944).

Also commentaries on the Revelation (chapter 20).

# KINGDOM

## KINGDOM in the Old Testament

The word "kingdom" is used 147 times in the Old Testament and appears also under the translations "reign," "realm," "royal," and "empire." The word is used 118 times in reference to kingdoms of the world: the kingdoms of Darius, Ahasuerus, Nebucharnezzar, Belshazzar, Saul, David, Solomon, etc. The remaining twenty-nine appearances of the words are used in two ways: (1) the rule of God over men (Dan. 4:17, 25, 34; 5:21; Ps. 103:19; 145:11-13); and (2) the Messianic kingdom which God will set up in the end times. The features of this kingdom are as follows:

1. God promised this kingdom, which would last "forever," to David (1 Chron. 17:11, 14; cf. Acts 2:29, 30).
2. God will set up this kingdom in the days of the last world kingdom (Dan. 2:44).
3. This kingdom will never be destroyed, but will abide forever (Dan. 2:44; 7:14).
4. This kingdom will consume and destroy the other kingdoms existing in the world at the end times (Dan. 2:44).
5. God will give this kingdom to the Son of man (Dan. 7:14).
6. All people, nations, and languages will constitute the kingdom (Dan. 7:14).

7. The saints of the Most High will possess the kingdom (Dan. 7:18, 22).

8. Righteousness will characterize the kingdom (Ps. 45:6; cf. Heb. 1:8).

## KINGDOM in the New Testament

The word "kingdom(s)" occurs 162 times in the New Testament (a.v.). Of these, 128 are in the four gospels alone. Many times the word appears with the qualifying phrases "of heaven" and "of God." The first of these, "kingdom of heaven," is used only by Matthew, where it appears thirty-two times. The other phrase, "kingdom of God," however, is used in all four gospels, as well as in other New Testament books: five times in Matthew; fifteen in Mark; thirty-three in Luke; two in John; and sixteen in the rest of the New Testament.

Apart from the qualifying expressions "of heaven" or "of God," the word "kingdom(s)" appears fifty-nine times in the New Testament. Five of these in Matthew, however, are used in the immediate context of "kingdom of heaven," and therefore, would indicate identity (8:12; 13:38, 41, 43; 25: 34). Two in Luke are also in contexts of "the kingdom of God," and would, therefore, indicate identity (19:12, 15). One in Acts 20:25, though rendered "kingdom of God" in the Authorized Version, omits the qualifying expression "of God" in the best manuscripts according to Nestle's Greek Testament. This has been rendered also as: (1) "kingdom of Jesus," supported by Codex Bezae, by a later European Latin manuscript (gig), by the Sahidic version, originating in Upper Egypt about A.D. 250, and by manuscript fragments dating from the fifth century onward; and (2) "kingdom of the Lord Jesus," supported by a later European manuscript (gig); and (3) "kingdom of God," supported by Codex H from the ninth century, by Codex L from the ninth century, by Codex E from the eighth century, by a mass of later manuscripts, by the Texts Receptus, by Luther's translation, and by the Vulgate. This textual evidence means that early translators considered these terms to refer to the same kingdom and hence to be used interchangeably.

A survey of the use of "kingdom(s)" in the New Testament apart from the expression "of heaven" and "of God" reveals the following:

1. It refers to kingdoms of the world (Matt. 4:8; 24:7; Heb. 11:33; Rev. 16:10; 17:12, 17, 18). The kingdoms of the world will become the kingdom of our Lord at the end of this age (Rev. 11:15).

2. It refers to God's rule: "thy kingdom come"; "thine is the kingdom" (Matt. 6:10, 13).

3. Jesus preached the gospel of the kingdom (Matt. 4:23; 9:35). The gospel of the kingdom will be preached in all the world for a witness before the end of the age (Matt. 24:14).

4. It is used in reference to Satan's kingdom (Matt. 12:25, 26).

5. The unrighteous do not inherit the kingdom (Eph. 5:5); the poor of this world are heirs (James 2:5).

6. The mother of Zebedee's children requested that her sons might sit on the right and left of the Lord in His kingdom (Matt. 20:20, 21).

7. The Lord will drink with His disciples once again the fruit of the vine in the Father's kingdom (Matt. 26:29).

8. The Lord will judge the quick and the dead at His appearing and His kingdom (2 Tim. 4:1). Righteousness is the scepter of His kingdom (Heb. 1:8).

9. Paul preached the kingdom and the grace of God to all at Ephesus (Acts 20:24, 25). He also told the Colossians that believers already have been translated into the kingdom (Col. 1:13). He told the Thessalonians that they were called unto His kingdom and glory (1 Thess. 2:12). He said that he would be preserved unto the Lord's heavenly kingdom (2 Tim. 4:18). He told the

Hebrews that they received a kingdom which cannot be moved (Heb. 12:28).

10. The Apostle Peter said that an entrance will be ministered to believers into the everlasting kingdom of our Lord and Savior Jesus Christ (2 Peter 1:11).

11. The Apostle John wrote to the believers of Asia Minor that he was a companion with them in the kingdom of Jesus Christ (Rev. 1:9).

12. After the last resurrection Christ will deliver the kingdom to the Father (1 Cor. 15:24).

**Kingdom Proclaimed by:**

1. John the Baptist (Matt. 3:2);
2. Jesus (Matt. 4:17; Mark 1:15; Luke 4:43; 8:1; 9:11; Acts 1:3-6);
3. The Twelve Apostles (Matt. 10:7; Luke 9:2; 10:9, 11);
4. The keys of the kingdom given to Peter (Matt. 16:19);
5. Those who would wholly follow Jesus (Luke 9:60);
6. Philip (Acts 8:12);
7. Paul at Ephesus (Acts 19:8); Paul at Rome (Acts 28: 23, 31).

**Kingdom Explained in Parables**

1. Disciples, not others, to know the mysteries of the kingdom (Matt. 13:11; Luke 8:10).
2. Kingdom like a man sowing seed (Matt. 13:24; Mark 4:26).
3. Kingdom like a mustard seed (Matt. 13:31; Mark 4:31; Luke 13:18, 19).
4. Kingdom like leaven in dough (Matt. 13:33; Luke 13: 20, 21).
5. Kingdom like hidden treasure (Matt. 13:44).
6. Kingdom of heaven like a pearl of great value (Matt. 13:45).
7. Kingdom of heaven like a net full of fish (Matt. 13:47).

8. Kingdom of heaven like a householder of new and old treasures (Matt. 13:52).
9. Kingdom of heaven like a king taking account of his servants (Matt. 18:23).
10. Kingdom of heaven like a householder who hired laborers to work in his vineyard (Matt. 20:1).
11. Kingdom of heaven like a king who invited guests to the marriage of his son (Matt. 22:2).
12. Kingdom of heaven like ten virgins meeting the bridegroom (Matt. 25:1).

## Conditions for Entrance into the Kingdom

1. Doing the will of the Father (Matt. 7:21).
2. Plucking out an eye to enter, if necessary (Mark 9:47).
3. Being converted and having the attitude of little children (Matt. 18:3; Mark 10:15; Luke 18:17).
4. Riches somehow hinder; the rich hardly enter the kingdom (Matt. 19:23, 24; Mark 10:23-25; Luke 18:24, 25).
5. Obedience to commandments is not far from entrance into the kingdom of God (Mark 12:34).
6. No man looking back is fit for the kingdom of God (Luke 9:62).
7. One should leave families for the kingdom's sake, if necessary (Luke 18:29).
8. New birth, of water and spirit, is necessary for entrance (John 3:3-5).
9. The kingdom of God is entered through much tribulation (Acts 14:22; cf. Rom. 5:3).
10. The unrighteous shall not inherit the kingdom of God (1 Cor. 6:9, 10; Gal. 5:21).
11. Flesh and blood cannot inherit the kingdom of God (1 Cor. 15:50).

## Those Who Gain the Kingdom

1. The poor in spirit (Matt. 5:3).
2. Those persecuted for righteousness' sake (Matt. 5:10).

3. Those who break God's commandments are least in the kingdom, whereas those who teach His commandments are great in the kingdom (Matt. 5:19).
4. Some disciples would see the kingdom come with power before their death (Mark 9:1).
5. Abraham, Isaac, Jacob, and all the prophets are in the kingdom; also many from the East and West, North and South, will sit down in the kingdom with them (Matt. 8:11; Luke 13:28, 29).
6. The least in the kingdom is greater than John the Baptist, the greatest born of women (Matt. 11:11; Luke 7:28).
7. Those with a humble attitude like children constitute the kingdom (Matt. 18:1, 4; 19:14; Mark 10:14; Luke 18:16).
8. Joseph of Arimathea waited for the kingdom (Mark 15:43; Luke 23:51).
9. Pharisees did not enter, and they hindered those who wanted to from entering (Matt. 23:13).
10. Publicans and harlots will enter before the chief priests and elders of Israel (Matt. 21:31).
11. Some who made themselves eunuchs for the kingdom's sake (Matt. 19:12).
12. Paul's fellow workers (Col. 4:11).
13. Thessalonians who suffered for the kingdom (2 Thess. 1:5). For others, see numbers 9, 10, 11 under KINGDOM IN THE NEW TESTAMENT.

## Nature of the Kingdom

1. The kingdom of God is not meat and drink, but righteousness, peace, and joy in the Holy Spirit (Rom. 14:17).
2. The kingdom of God is not in word, but in power (1 Cor. 4:20).
3. Blessed is the man who eats bread in the kingdom of God (Luke 14:15).

4. The Kingdom is not political in nature: "Jesus answered, 'My kingdom is not of this world; if my kingdom were of this world, then would my servants fight, that I should not be delivered to the Jews: but now is my kingdom not from hence'" (John 18:36).

## Time of the Realization of the Kingdom

1. In the present. The Pharisees asked when the kingdom of God should come. Jesus answered that it comes "not with observation," but is *within you*" (Luke 17:21).
2. In the future. The Lord will eat meat and drink of the fruit of the vine in the kingdom of God *at His return* (Mark 14:25; Luke 22:16, 18).
3. People thought the kingdom should appear at the time when Christ came to Jerusalem (Luke 19:11).
4. The kingdom of God is near when signs in the sun and moon appear at Christ's second coming (Luke 21:31).
5. The kingdom of heaven comes when the accuser of the brethren is cast out of heaven (Rev. 12:10).

## Different Interpretations of the Kingdom

Some interpreters hold that a literal, earthly, political, Messianic kingdom was offered by Christ at His first coming. They hold that Christ came first to Israel as King. The Jews, however, rejected the kingdom and crucified the King. Whereupon the kingdom was postponed and held in abeyance until the second coming of Christ when it will be realized. Those who hold this view affirm the Scriptures to teach the following:

1. The Jews expected such a kingdom.

   And, behold, there was a man in Jerusalem, whose name was Simeon; and the same man was just and devout, waiting for *the consolation of Israel:* and the Holy Ghost was upon him (Luke 2:25).

2. Circumstances attending Christ's birth indicated His coming as King.

Where is he that is born *King of the Jews?* for we have seen his star in the east, and are come to worship him (Matt. 2:2).

He shall be great, and shall be called the Son of the Highest: and the Lord God shall give unto him *the throne of his father David;* and *he shall reign over the house of Jacob for ever;* and of his kingdom there shall be no end (Luke 1:32, 33).

And his father Zachariah was filled with the Holy Ghost, and prophesied, saying, Blessed be the Lord God of Israel; for he hath visited and redeemed his people (Luke 1:67, 68).

3. John the Baptist, Christ, and His disciples, preached the kingdom as "at hand."

4. The kingdom message was not to be proclaimed to the Gentiles.

These twelve Jesus sent forth, and commanded them, saying, Go not into the way of the Gentiles, and into any city of the Samaritans enter ye not: but go rather to the lost sheep of the house of Israel (Matt. 10:5, 6).

But he answered and said, I am not sent but unto the lost sheep of the house of Israel (Matt. 15:24).

Now I say that Jesus Christ was a minister of the circumcision for the truth of God, to confirm the promises made unto the fathers (Rom. 15:8).

5. The triumphal entry into Jerusalem was the prophetic fulfillment of the coming of the Messianic King (Matt. 21:4, 5, 9; Zech. 9:9). Although He had already been rejected, this official offer of a kingdom, in fulfillment of Old Testament prophecy, was "another opportunity" for the nation to accept the King (Matt. 11:20-30; 12:14-21; John 6:66; 18:39, 40).

6. When Christ and His offer of the kingdom were rejected by Israel, the realization of the kingdom was postponed and is now being held in abeyance, in mystery form.

That it might be fulfilled which was spoken by the prophet, saying, I will open my mouth in parables; I will utter things which have been kept secret from the foundation of the world (Matt. 13:35).

7. When Christ and His offer of the kingdom were rejected, He began to speak to His disciples of His death.

From that time forth began Jesus to shew unto his disciples, how that he must go unto Jerusalem, and suffer many things of the elders and chief priests, and scribes, and be killed, and be raised again the third day (Matt. 16:21).

And Jesus going up to Jerusalem took the twelve disciples apart in the way, and said unto them, Behold, we go up to Jerusalem; and the Son of man shall be betrayed unto the chief priests and unto the scribes, and they shall condemn him to death (Matt. 20:17, 18).

8. Upon His rejection by Israel Christ also announced His purpose in building the Church and His turning to the Gentiles with salvation, which purpose was not revealed before in Old Testament times.

The Bible teachers who hold the "postponement theory" make a distinction between the terms "kingdom of heaven" and "kingdom of God." They interpret the "kingdom of heaven" as the Messianic rule of Christ and the "kingdom of God" as the larger sphere of God's sovereign rule in the universe. The kingdom of God includes His rule in the hearts of the redeemed. The kingdom of God, as such, is described in Romans 14:17 as being a state of "righteousness, peace and joy in the Holy Ghost, "the new birth being necessary for entrance" (John 3:3, 5).

These Bible teachers state that Christ's offer of a kingdom to Israel was a "bona fide" offer. Had He been accepted as King, the promised Davidic kingdom would have been set up. The question arises that if Christ had thus been accepted, how then could He become the rejected, crucified Redeemer of the world? To this question two answers are given: (1) God in His foreknowledge knew that Christ would be rejected and that a redemption would be realized which would also bring salvation to the Gentiles; or, (2) God never intended the cross in the first place, but would have provided salvation through the Jewish system of sacrifice. (S. D. Gordon)

Contrary to this interpretation, other Bible teachers hold that Christ had no intention of setting up an earthly political kingdom at His first coming, but that He came the first time to offer salvation to Jew and Gentile alike, and to become the Lamb of God that takes away the sin of the world. At His *second coming* Christ will establish an earthly, political kingdom which will be the material realization of the kingdom promised in the Old Testament. Christ will then reign in His kingdom with those who have followed Him in the regeneration (Matt. 19:28; 2 Tim. 2:12). Those who hold this interpretation affirm the Scriptures to teach the following:

1. The present state of the kingdom of God is a spiritual one of righteousness, peace, and joy in the Holy Spirit.

    For the kingdom of God is not meat and drink; but righteousness, and peace, and joy in the Holy Ghost (Rom. 14: 17).

    Jesus answered, My kingdom is not of this world: if my kingdom were of this world, then would my servants fight, that I should not be delivered to the Jews: but now is my kingdom not from hence (John 18:36).

    Who hath delivered us from the power of darkness, and hath translated us into the kingdom of his dear Son (Col. 1:13).

2. John the Baptist, Christ, and His disciples at His first coming preached repentance as necessary for entrance into the kingdom.

    Repent ye: for the kingdom of heaven is at hand (Matt. 3:2).

    Except a man be born again, he cannot see the kingdom of God. . . . Except a man be born of water and of the Spirit, he cannot enter into the kingdom of God (John 3: 3, 5).

3. This kingdom of salvation was offered to all, being pro-

claimed to Israel first because they were Christ's own kindred in the flesh and bearers of the promises.

For mine eyes have seen thy salvation, which thou hast prepared before the face of all people; a light to lighten the Gentiles, and the glory of thy people Israel (Luke 2:30-32).

These twelve Jesus sent forth, and commanded them, saying, Go not into the way of the Gentiles and into any city of the Samaritans enter ye not, but go rather to the lost sheep of the house of Israel (Matt. 10:5, 6).

And many of the Samaritans of that city believed on him for the saying of the woman, which testified, He told me all that ever I did. So when the Samaritans were come unto him, they besought him that he would tarry with them; and he abode there two days. And many believed because of his own word; and said unto the woman, Now we believe, not because of thy saying: for we have heard him ourselves, and know that this is indeed the Christ, the Saviour of the world (John 4:39-42).

And other sheep I have, which are not of this fold: them also I must bring, and they shall hear my voice; and there shall be one fold, and one shepherd (John 10:16).

Who are Israelites; to whom pertaineth the adoption, and the glory, and the covenants, and the giving of the law, and the service of God, and the promises; whose are the fathers, and of whom as concerning the flesh Christ came (Rom. 9:4, 5).

For the Scripture saith, Whosoever believeth on him shall not be ashamed. For there is no difference between the Jew and the Greek: for the same Lord over all is rich unto all that call upon him. For whosoever shall call upon the name of the Lord shall be saved (Rom. 10:11-13).

And he said, It is a light thing that thou shouldest be my servant to raise up the tribes of Jacob, and to restore the preserved of Israel: I will also give thee for a light to the Gentiles, that thou mayest be my salvation unto the end of the earth (Isa. 49:6).

4. The terms "kingdom of heaven" and "kingdom of God" are used interchangeably. The following is the comparative use of the two expressions in the Synoptic Gospels:

| Matthew | Mark | Luke |
|---|---|---|
| Jesus preached the "kingdom of heaven" as at hand (4:17). | Jesus preached the "kingdom of God" as at hand (1:15). | |
| Parable of Sower describes "kingdom of heaven" (13:11). | Both Mark and Luke record the Parable of the Sower as a description of the "kingdom of God" (Mark 4:11; Luke 8:10). | |
| "Kingdom of heaven" likened to grain of mustard seed (13:31). | Both Mark and Luke compare the "kingdom of God" to a grain of mustard seed (Mark 4:30; Luke 13:18). | |
| "Kingdom of heaven" likened to leaven (13:33). | | "Kingdom of God" likened to leaven (13:20). |
| Concerning His transfiguration, Jesus said that some would not taste of death until they saw the Son of man coming in "his kingdom" (16:28). | Both Mark and Luke wrote that Jesus said they would not taste of death until they saw the "kingdom of God" come (Mark 9:1; Luke 9:27). | |
| Better to enter "into life" with only one eye than having two eyes to be cast into hell (18:9). | Better to enter the "kingdom of God" with one eye, than having two eyes to be cast in hell fire (9:47). | |
| Suffer little children to come, for of such is "the kingdom of heaven" (19:14). | Both Mark and Luke record Jesus as saying: ". . . for of such is the kingdom of God." (Mark 10:14; Luke 18:16). | |
| "Except ye be converted and become as little children, ye shall not enter the "kingdom of heaven" (18:3). | Both Mark and Luke record Jesus as saying: "Whosoever shall not receive the kingdom of God as a little child, he shall not enter therein" (Mark 10:15; Luke 18:17). | |
| That a rich man shall hardly enter the "kingdom of heaven" (19:23). It is easier for a camel to go through the eye of a needle, than for a rich man to enter into the "kingdom of God" (19:24). | Both Mark and Luke expressed the same difficulty of rich men in entering the "kingdom of God" (Mark 10:23; Luke 18:24). | |

| Matthew | Mark | Luke |
|---|---|---|
| Christ said He would not drink of the vine until "the kingdom of my Father" (26:29). | Both Mark and Luke recorded Christ as saying He would not drink of the vine until "the kingdom of God" (Mark 14:25; Luke 22:18). | |
| Reward for the poor in spirit is the "kingdom of heaven" (5:3). | | Reward for the poor in spirit is the "kingdom of God" (6:20). |
| Least in "kingdom of heaven" is greater than John the Baptist (11:11). | | Least in "kingdom of God" is greater than John the Baptist (7:28). |
| Jesus commissioned the disciples to preach the "kingdom of heaven" (10:7). | | Jesus commissioned them to preach the "kingdom of God" (9:2). |
| Seek first "kingdom" and his righteousness (Greek text, 6:33). | | Seek "his kingdom" (Greek text, 12:31). |
| (The A.V. reads "kingdom of God" for both Matthew and Luke. However, Nestle's Greek Testament, according to the best manuscript evidence contains the above readings.) | | |
| Many shall sit with Abraham, Isaac, and Jacob in the "kingdom of heaven" (8:11, 12). | | Same, but with "kingdom of God" (13:28). |
| "Kingdom of heaven" suffers violence from the days of John the Baptist (11:12). | | "Kingdom of God" pressed into since the time of John the Baptist (16:16). |
| | No one has left father, mother, children or field "for the sake of my name and the gospel" but he shall receive an hundredfold (19:29). | Same as Mark, but substitutes "for the sake of the kingdom of God" (18:29). |

5. This kingdom will be realized in an earthly, political sense at the second coming of Christ.

When the Son of man shall come in his glory, and all the

holy angels with him, then shall he sit upon the throne of his glory (Matt. 25:31).

He said therefore, A certain nobleman went into a far country to receive for himself a kingdom, and to return. . . . And it came to pass, that when he was returned, having received the kingdom . . . (Luke 19:12-15).

˙So likewise ye, when ye see these things come to pass. know ye that the kingdom of God is nigh at hand (Luke 21:31).

I charge thee therefore before God, and the Lord Jesus Christ, who shall judge the quick and the dead at his appearing and his kingdom (2 Tim. 4:1).

And the seventh angel sounded; and there were great voices in heaven, saying, The kingdoms of this world are become the kingdom of our Lord, and of his Christ; and he shall reign for ever and ever (Rev. 11:15).

## Bibliography

Berkhof, Louis. *The Kingdom of God.* Grand Rapids, Michigan: William B. Eerdmans, 1951.

Bright, John. *The Kingdom of God.* New York: Abingdon-Cokesbury Press, 1953.

Brock, A. Clutton. *What Is the Kingdom of Heaven?* New York: Charles Scribner's Sons, 1920.

Chafer, Lewis Sperry. *The Kingdom in History and Prophecy.* Chicago: Moody Press, 1936.

Govett, R. *Entrance Into the Kingdom.* London: Charles J. Thynne, 1922.

Ladd, George. *Crucial Questions About the Kingdom of God.* Grand Rapids, Michigan: William B. Eerdmans, 1952.

─────. "The Kingdom of God in the Jewish Apocryphal Literature," *Bibliotheca Sacra,* 109:55-62 (January, 1952).

─────. "The Kingdom of God in I Enoch," *Bibliotheca Sacra,* 110:32-49 (January, 1953).

McClain, Alva J. *The Greatness of the Kingdom.* Grand Rapids, Michigan: Zondervan Publishing House, 1959.

Walden, J. W. "The Kingdom of God — Its Millennial Dispensations," *Bibliotheca Sacra,* 102:433-41 (October, 1945); 103:39-49 (January, 1946).

Walvoord, John F. "The Kingdom Promised to David," *Bibliotheca Sacra,* 110:97-110 (April, 1953).

─────. "A Review of 'Crucial Questions About the Kingdom of God,'" *Bibliotheca Sacra,* 110:437 (January, 1953).

Wyngaarden, M. J. *The Future of the Kingdom in Prophecy and Fulfillment.* Grand Rapids, Michigan: Zondervan Publishing House, 1934.

# CHURCH

THE CHURCH IS THE KINGDOM OF REGENERATED
BELIEVERS "CALLED OUT" OF THE WORLD. —— COL.1:13
I THESS.2:12, I COR.12:13, EPH.4:4, ROM.12:5

"THEN
SHALL THE
RIGHTEOUS
SHINE
FORTH AS
THE SUN
IN THE
KINGDOM
OF THE
FATHER".
———
MATT.13:43
I COR.15:24
LUKE 13:29

# KINGDOM OF GOD

BEGAN
AT
PENTECOST
ACTS 2:1,41,47

70 A.D.

THE
SON OF MAN
COMING
IN HIS
KINGDOM

LUKE 21:27,31
MATT.13:41

RAPTURE

"THIS GOSPEL OF THE KINGDOM SHALL BE PREACHED
IN ALL THE WORLD FOR A WITNESS UNTO ALL
NATIONS; THEN SHALL THE END COME." —— MATT.24:14

"I WILL BUILD
MY CHURCH"
MATT.16:18,21

MATT.20:28
MARK 10:45
JOHN 12:27
JOHN 18:36:37

"THE TIME
OF THY
VISITATION"

MATT.21:4-5
MATT.23:37-39
LUKE 19:41-44
———
MATT.21:43

"THE KINGDOM
OF HEAVEN
SUFFERETH
VIOLENCE"

MATT.11:12
MATT.13:25
JOHN 6:15

JOHN
THE
BAPTIST

MATT.3:2
MATT.4:17
MATT.10:7

THE
LAW
AND
THE
PROPHETS
WERE
UNTIL
JOHN
———
LUKE 16:16

A STUDY OF

# THE CHURCH AND KINGDOM

IN THE NEW TESTAMENT

# WORLD CONDITIONS
# IN THE LAST TIMES

## BIBLICAL REFERENCES

The following passages describe world conditions prevailing at the time of our Lord's return. The full meaning of key words will be given after each reference.

### 1. Matthew 24:37-39 (cf. Luke 17:26-30)

> But as the days of Noah were, so shall also the coming of the Son of man be. For as in the days that were before the flood they were eating and drinking, marrying and giving in marriage, until the day that Noah entered into the ark, and knew not until the flood came, and took them all away; so shall also the coming of the Son of man be.

*"Eating, drinking, marrying."*

There is no idea of excess inherent in these words in the original Greek. The words "eating" and "drinking" are the common terms used for nourishing the body (Thayer). They are also used in the passages referring to the Lord's supper (John 6:54): "Whoso eateth my flesh and drinketh. . ."; ". . . and he took the cup . . . saying, Drink ye all of it" (Matt. 26:27). The word for "marrying" is the same used of the marriage in Cana which the Lord attended.

It seems that the above text, therefore, simply teaches the suddenness of His return. No one will know the day or hour, but will be occupied in the ordinary things of life. One may interpret that the passages reveal carelessness and a lack of watchfulness for His return. Those living at the time will be so busy with the "cares of this life" that the day of His return will come upon them unawares (Luke 21:34).

## 2. Luke 18:8

Nevertheless, when the Son of man cometh, shall he find (the) faith on the earth?

*"The faith."*

In the margin of the Revised Version and in Nestle's Greek Testament the article "the" is added, making faith definite as "the faith." Since this verse appears in the story of the importunate widow, it may mean: (1) that the Lord will not find "faith which has endured in prayer without fainting," as exemplified in the importunate widow; or (2) that the Lord will not find faith that brings salvation when He comes again.

## 3. 1 Thessalonians 5:2, 3

For yourselves know perfectly that the day of the Lord so cometh as a thief in the night. For when they shall say, Peace and safety; then sudden destruction cometh upon them, as travail upon a woman with child; and they shall not escape.

*"Sudden destruction."*

The destruction described is unexpected and unforeseen. The Greek word for "sudden" is also translated "unawares" in Luke 21:34: "And take heed to yourselves, lest at any time your hearts be overcharged with surfeiting, and drunkenness, and cares of this life, and so that day come upon you unawares." "Destruction" means ultimate ruin and death out of which they will not be able to flee.

## 4. 2 Thessalonians 2:3

For that day shall not come, except there come a (the) falling away first, and that man of sin be revealed, the son of perdition.

*"The falling away."*

The definite article is used in the Revised Version, based on the Greek text. The Greek verb, "falling away," is sometimes translated in the New Testament as "depart" as well as "fall away." Hence, the passage may be interpreted as: (1) "the falling away" from the faith, as used in 1 Timothy 4:1, describing a condition of apostasy or apathy as preceding the revelation of the man of sin; or (2) as a "departing," and thus may refer to the departure of the church before the revelation of the man of sin. This would then be in accord with the statement in verse 7.

### 5. 1 Timothy 4:1, 2

> Now the Spirit speaketh expressly, that in the latter times some shall depart from the faith, giving heed to seducing spirits, and doctrines of devils; speaking lies in hypocrisy; having their conscience seared with a hot iron.

*"Depart."*

The departing from the faith mentioned here is literally "the standing away from" or "falling away from" the faith, as used in 2 Thessalonians 2:3 above.

*"Giving heed."*

In the last times continuous attention will be paid to seducing spirits.

*"Seducing spirits."*

These seducing spirits will "deceive"; "mislead"; "cause to wander into error and delusion." The word "seducing" is used elsewhere in reference to: (1) deceivers who confess not that Jesus Christ is come in the flesh. This is a deceiver (i.e. "one who seduces") and an antichrist, says the Apostle John (2 John 7); (2) antichrists and false prophets who deceive by word of mouth as well as by signs, wonders, and miracles (Matt. 24:5, 11, 24; 2 Peter 2:18); (3) those who say they have not sinned, a delusion which is of the same seducing spirit that denies that Jesus is the Christ (1 John 1:8); (4) Satan himself as the great Dragon and old Serpent which deceives the whole world (Rev. 20:3).

### "Doctrines of devils."

Continuous attention will also be given to demonic doctrines and teachings prevailing in the last times.

### "Speaking lies in hypocrisy."

People will be pretenders to truth and piety.

### "Conscience seared with a hot iron."

They will have consciences with no moral standards and no feeling, as flesh burned with a branding iron (Thayer).

### 6. 2 Timothy 3:1-5

> This know also, that in the last days perilous times shall come. For men shall be lovers of their own selves, covetous, boasters, proud, blasphemers, disobedient to parents, unthankful, unholy, without natural affection, trucebreakers, false accusers, incontinent, fierce, despisers of those that are good, traitors, heady, highminded, lovers of pleasures more than lovers of God; having a form of godliness, but denying the power thereof: from such turn away.

### "Perilous."

This word describes times of annoyance and oppression that will be troublesome, dangerous, and hard to bear. This adjective is used in only one other place in the New Testament — Matthew 8:28. There it describes the two possessed of demons in the country of the Gergesenes "coming out of the tombs, exceeding *fierce,* so that no man might pass by that way."

### "Lovers of their own selves."

This phrase is one word in the original and appears nowhere else in the New Testament.

*"Covetous."*

That is, loving money.

*"Boasters."*

This word, meaning "empty pretenders," is also used in Romans 1:30 in reference to those who oppose God. The noun form of the word, "boastings," is used as that which is not of the Father, but of the world: ". . . the lust of the flesh, and the lust of the eyes, and the pride ('boasting') of life, is not of the Father, but is of the world" (1 John 2:16).

*"Proud."*

The idea expressed in this word is that of showing one's self above others with an arrogant estimate of one's own means or merits. The word is used in the New Testament only in a bad sense. God is always against the proud (James 4:6).

*"Blasphemers."*

This means simply "evil speakers."

*"Unholy."*

This means to be impious, wicked, or irreligious. How contrary to Paul's admonition: "I will therefore that men pray everywhere, lifting up holy hands, without wrath and doubting."

*"Without natural affection."*

This means that there will be an absence of love and affection among family or kindred.

*"Trucebreakers."*

These are people who cannot even be persuaded to make a promise, according to the root idea of the word, "implacable."

*"False accusers."*

This word, meaning "slanderers," is used almost exclusively of Satan in the New Testament. It is our English word "devil." Its use here would suggest that people in the last times would act the part of Satan or be in accord with him in opposing the cause of God.

*"Incontinent."*

That is, without the power of self-control; intemperate.

*"Fierce."*

This term denotes that which is savage and beastly. The people of the last times have thrown over the restraints of the civilized and humane man in favor of the impulsive and instinctive habits of animals.

*"Despisers of those that are good."*

This phrase refers to those who are opposed to goodness and good men.

*"Traitors."*

"Betrayers." The word appears elsewhere in the New Testament with reference to the betraying of Christ by Judas.

*"Heady."*

This term means rash or reckless or impulsive. The word is used also of the impulsive disturbance caused by the silversmiths at Ephesus (Acts 19:36).

*"Highminded."*

This word means properly "to raise a smoke" or "to wrap in a mist," and hence "to puff up and becloud with pride." The people of the last times are not in contact with reality because they are "beclouded with pride."

*"Lovers of pleasure."*

This is the only appearance of the word "lovers" in the New Testament. The word "pleasure," however, is used in Luke 8:14 as referring to that which choked the good seed of the kingdom and prevented it from bearing fruit. Hence, its use here would suggest that in the last times people will be lovers of those things which choke the gospel message. The same word "pleasure" is translated "lusts" in James 4:1 where it refers to the causes of inter-personal conflict.

*"Having a form of godliness but denying the power thereof."*

People appear to be religious, but are not in reality, having renounced the power or worth of religion.

*"From these turn away."*

That the apostle would admonish those to whom he was writing in his own day to "turn away" from people like these described would indicate that while these are conditions of the last times, they were in some respects also conditions of the apostle's own day.

### 7. 2 Timothy 4:3, 4

> For the time will come when they will not endure sound doctrine; but after their own lusts shall they heap to themselves teachers, having itching ears; and they shall turn away their ears from the truth and shall be turned unto fables.

*"They will not endure sound doctrine."*

The word "endure" means "to hold one's self firm and erect," and describes people who will not take a definite stand for the things of Chirst. How like the attitude of many who disregard wholesome ("sound") truth and who declare the preaching of doctrine to be unessential! How contrary to the admonitions in 2 Timothy 1:13 and Titus 1:9: "Hold fast the form of sound words which thou hast heard of me. . . ."

*"Turned aside to fables."*

This is i.e. to the fictitious and legendary.

### 8. 2 Peter 3:3, 4

> Knowing this first, that there shall come in the last days scoffers, walking after their own lusts, and saying, Where

is the promise of his coming? for since the fathers fell asleep, all things continue as they were from the beginning of the creation?

*"Scoffers."*

They are, i.e. "mockers" or "triflers who play like children," not minding serious things, but who walk according to their own desires and ideas of the Lord's return.

*"After their own lusts."*

Sensual cravings and longings (cf. Jude 18).

(The above studies are based on Thayer's *Greek-English Lexicon of the New Testament* and Wigram's *The Englishman's Greek Concordance of the New Testament*.)

## Bibliography

Andrews, Samuel J. *Christianity and Anti-Christianity in Their Final Conflict*. Chicago: Moody Bible Institute, 1898.

Cooper, David L. *Preparing for the World-wide Revival*. Los Angeles. The Biblical Research Society, 1938.

Gaebelein, Arno C. *As It Was — So Shall It Be*. New York: Our Hope, 1937.

Lindsey, Hal. *The Late Great Planet Earth*. Grand Rapids, Michigan: Zondervan Publishing House, 1970.

Munro, John Ker. "The Signs of the Times," *Bibliotheca Sacra*, 96:224-42 (April, 1939).

Scofield, C. I. "The Course and End of the Age," *Bibliotheca Sacra*, 108: 105-16 (January, 1951).

# MILLENNIUM

The millennium is a period of a thousand years mentioned in Revelation 20:2-7. This passage reveals the following facts concerning the millennium:

1. Satan is bound and sealed in the bottomless pit during the millennium.
2. John saw a group sitting upon thrones, to whom judgment was given, and also the souls of them that were beheaded for the witness of Jesus, and also those who had not worshiped the beast nor his image, neither had received his mark on their foreheads, or in their hands. These groups lived and reigned with Christ for a thousand years. This is the first resurrection.
3. The first resurrection precedes the millennium.
4. The second death has no power over those who have a part in the first resurrection.
5. The partakers of the second resurrection do not live until after the millennium.
6. Satan will be loosed after the thousand years for a little season.
7. The rebellion of Gog and Magog, inspired by Satan, follows the millennium.

This passage (Rev. 20:2-7) has been the subject of a great deal of theological controversy, and it has suggested three interpretations: postmillennialism, amillennialism, and premillennialism.

## Bibliography

Glasson, T. Francis. *His Appearing and His Kingdom.* London: Epworth, 1953.

MacRae, Allen A. "The Millennial Kingdom of Christ," *Our Hope,* 53: 463-80 (February, 1947).

Walvoord, John C. "The Millennial Issue in Modern Theology," *Bibliotheca Sacra,* 106:34-47 (January, 1949).

West, Nathaniel. *The Thousand Years in Both Testaments.* New York: Fleming H. Revell, 1880.

# POSTMILLENNIALISM

### Definition

As illustrated by the following diagram, postmillennialism is a theological position that affirms the second coming of Christ to be *post-* or *after* the millennial period.

### Method of Scripture Interpretation

Postmillenarians hold to a symbolic interpretation of Scripture text. The Old Testament prophecies concerning Israel and the Kingdom, for instance, are spiritually realized and fulfilled in the Church of the New Testament. The symbolic method of interpreting is held to be legitimate because:

1. *Figurative language is used in the Scriptures.*

   The mountains and the hills shall break forth before you into singing, and all the trees of the field shall clap their hands (Isa. 55:12).

2. *Old Testament prophecies are spiritually understood in the New Testament.*

   And if ye be Christ's, then are ye Abraham's seed, and heirs according to the promise. (The Gentile Galatians who had become Christians are considered descendants of Abraham, not literally of course, but spiritually.) (Gal. 3: 29).

For he is not a Jew, which is one outwardly; neither is that circumcision, which is outward in the flesh; but he is a Jew, which is one inwardly; and circumcision is that of the heart, in the spirit, and not in the letter (Rom. 2: 28, 29).

For we are the circumcision, which worship God in the spirit, and rejoice in Christ Jesus, and have no confidence in the flesh (Phil. 3:3).

3. *Scripture itself contains allegories: Galatians 4:21-31.*

### Nature of the Millennium and Its Relation to World History

Postmillenarians affirm the millennium to be a literal period of a thousand years of peace and righteousness in this age preceding the second coming of Christ. The millennial period is characterized by:

1. *Universal peace and righteousness.*

And many nations shall come and say, Come, and let us go up to the mountain of the Lord, and to the house of the God of Jacob; and he will teach us of his ways, and we will walk in his paths: for the law shall go forth out of Zion, and the word of the Lord from Jerusalem. And he shall judge among many people, and rebuke strong nations afar off, and they shall beat thir swords into plowshares, and their spears into pruninghooks; nation shall not lift up a sword against nation, neither shall they learn war any more (Micah 4:2, 3).

2. *Universal preaching and reception of the Gospel.*

For the earth shall be full of the knowledge of the Lord, as the waters cover the sea (Isa. 11:9).

And it shall be said in that day, Lo, this is our God; we have waited for him, and he will save us; this is the Lord: we have waited for him, we will be glad and rejoice in his salvation (Isa. 25:9).

And it shall come to pass, that from one new moon to another, and from one sabbath to another, shall all flesh come to worship before me, saith the Lord (Isa. 66:23).

3. *An unusual realization of the kingdom of God.*

a. Nature of the Kingdom.

Postmillenarians believe that the kingdom of God is a state of society in which the will of God is done in the hearts of "born-again" believers. This kingdom is spiritual since Christ Himself said that His kingdom is not of this world or His servants would fight for it (John 18:36) and that the condition of entrance is the new birth (John 3:3, 5; Matt. 18:3; Col. 1:13, 14). The kingdom of God is a state of righteousness, peace, and joy in the Holy Spirit (Rom. 14:17). No distinction is made between the kingdom of heaven, kingdom of God, kingdom of Christ, and the body of Christ; they all refer to the same rule of Christ in the hearts of believers.

b. Establishment of the kingdom.

Postmillenarians hold that the kingdom of God has been in existence from the beginning of the world. Christ came to reveal it more clearly and to extend it throughout the world.

c. Growth of the kingdom.

The kingdom is extended by the preaching of the Gospel, by the use of the church's ordinances of baptism and the Lord's Supper, and by other agencies of the organized church which are energized by the Holy Spirit.

> And this gospel of the kingdom shall be preached in all the world for a witness unto all nations; and then shall the end come (Matt. 24:14).
>
> Not by might, nor by power, but by my spirit, saith the Lord of hosts (Zech. 4:6).
>
> For if I go not away, the Comforter will not come unto you; but if I depart, I will send him unto you. And when he is come, he will reprove the world of sin, and of righteousness, and of judgment (John 16:7, 8).

The growth of the kingdom will be mixed, as illustrated by the parable of the wheat and tares (Matt. 13:24-30).

It will be extensive, as illustrated by the parables of the leaven and of the mustard seed (Matt. 13:31-33). It will be long and slow (Matt. 25:19; 2 Peter 3:8, 9). It will be attended with great crises, yet these will never break the principle of continuity (John 16:33).

d. The final form of the kingdom.

Postmillenarians affirm that this growth will continue until the world is practically Christianized. Evil will not be wholly eradicated from the world even at the height of this period, nor will the world under the preaching of the gospel be converted down to the very last man, but the world will become a great field of good grain, though mingled with some tares of evil. At the very end of this period there will be a reactionary outbreak of wickedness known as the period of the Great Tribulation.

### Relation of the Millennium to the Binding of Satan

During this millennial period of gospel prevalence, Satan will be bound. The binding of Satan has already taken place in the measure that the Gospel influence has spread throughout the world. The initial binding of Satan was announced by our Lord.

> But if I cast out devils by the Spirit of God, then the kingdom of God is come unto you. Or else how can one enter into a strong man's house, and spoil his goods, except he first bind the strong man? (Matt. 12:28, 29).

> And when he is come, he will reprove the world . . . of judgment, because the prince of this world is judged (John 16:8, 11).

> Now is the judgment of this world: now shall the prince of this world be cast out (John 12:31).

> . . . that through death he might destroy him that had the power of death, that is, the devil (Heb. 2:14).

> And having spoiled principalities and powers, he made a shew of them openly, triumphing over them in it (Col. 2: 15).

The binding of Satan will be realized in its most complete sense during the millennium (Rev. 20:2, 3).

### Relation of the Millennium to the Jews

Postmillenarians believe that the Jews will be converted either at the beginning, or sometime during, the thousand years, as stated in:

> And I will pour upon the house of David, and upon the inhabitants of Jerusalem, the spirit of grace and of supplications: and they shall look upon me whom they have pierced, and they shall mourn for him as one mourneth for his only son (Zech. 12:10).

> And so all Israel shall be saved: as it is written, There shall come out of Zion the Deliverer, and shall turn away ungodliness from Jacob: for this is my covenant unto them, when I shall take away their sins (Rom. 11:26, 27).

There will be no national regathering of Israel to Palestine in literal fulfillment of Old Testament prophecies. Their return is merely an accident of history. Christ's kingdom, being spiritual, is not confined to the Jew alone. Converted Gentiles are also to be "sons of the kingdom."

> And I say unto you, That many shall come from the east and west, and shall sit down with Abraham, and Isaac, and Jacob, in the kingdom of heaven (Matt. 8:11).

> And the Lord shall be known to Egypt, and the Egyptians shall know the Lord in that day, and shall do sacrifice and oblation; yea, they shall vow a vow unto the Lord, and perform it (Isa. 19:21).

> Even them (the sons of strangers) will I bring to my holy mountain, and make them joyful in my house of prayer: their burnt offerings and their sacrifices shall be accepted upon mine altar; for mine house shall be called an house of prayer for all people. The Lord God which gathereth the outcasts of Israel saith, Yet will I gather others to him, beside those that are gathered unto him (Isa. 56:7, 8).

> For from the rising of the sun even unto the going down of the same my name shall be great among the Gentiles; and in every place incense shall be offered unto my name,

> and a pure offering; for my name shall be great among
> the heathen, saith the Lord of Hosts (Mal. 1:11).

## The body of Christ is one, consisting of both Jew and Gentile.

> As thou hast given him power over all flesh, that he should
> give eternal life to as many as thou hast given him. . . .
> Neither pray I for these alone, but for them also which
> shall believe on me through their word, that they all may
> be one . . . even as we are one (John 17:2, 20, 22).
>
> For the scripture saith, Whosoever believeth on him shall
> not be ashamed, For there is no difference between the
> Jew and the Greek: for the same Lord over all is rich unto
> all that call upon him. For whosoever shall call upon the
> name of the Lord shall be saved (Rom. 10:11-13).

## Not Israel as a nation has a future history, but only the Israel of God which is one and the same as the Church.

> There is neither Jew nor Greek, there is neither bond nor
> free, there is neither male nor female; for ye are all one in
> Christ Jesus. And if ye be Christ's, then are ye Abraham's
> seed, and heirs according to the promise (Gal. 3:28, 29).

### Relation of the Millennium to the Great Tribulation

At the end of this millennial period and just before the
second coming of Christ (see chart), Satan will be loosed
for a little season. There will be a brief period of apostasy
and violent conflict between the kingdoms of light and
darkness.

> And when the thousand years are expired, Satan shall be
> loosed out of his prison, and shall go out to deceive the
> nations . . . (Rev. 20:7, 8).
>
> And this gospel of the kingdom shall be preached in all the
> world for a witness unto all nations; and then shall the
> end come. . . . For then shall be great tribulation, such
> as was not since the beginning of the world to this time,
> no, nor even shall be (Matt. 24:14, 21).
>
> Now the Spirit speaketh expressly, that in the latter times
> some shall depart from the faith . . . (1 Tim. 4:1-3).

### Relation of the Millennium to the Second Coming, Resurrection, Judgment, and Final Consummation

Postmillenarians hold that Christ will return at the close of this millennial period after a brief period of tribulation. At His coming there will be a general resurrection. The whole Church of God will be "made alive" at once, their "mortality being swallowed up of life."

> For as in Adam all die, even so in Christ shall all be made alive. But every man in his own order: Christ the first-fruits; afterward they that are Christ's at his coming. Then cometh the end, when he shall have delivered up the kingdom to God, even the Father (1 Cor. 15:22-24).

Christ will also deliver up the kingdom to the Father, and the "righteous ones will shine forth as the sun in the kingdom of their Father" (Matt. 13:43). The wicked will also be resurrected and will be judged together with the righteous at the second coming.

> For the Son of man shall come in the glory of his Father with his angels; and then he shall reward every man according to his works (Matt. 16:27).
>
> When the Son of man shall come in his glory, and all the holy angels with him, then shall he sit upon the throne of his glory: and before him shall be gathered all nations: and he shall separate them one from another, as a shepherd divideth his sheep from the goats (Matt. 25:31, 32; cf. Rev. 20:11-15).

The present earth and heaven will be dissolved by fire, giving way to a new heaven and a new earth which will be characterized by righteousness, unalloyed by any evil.

> But the day of the Lord shall come as a thief in the night; in the which the heavens shall pass away with a great noise, and the elements shall melt with fervent heat, the earth also and the works that are therein shall be burned up (2 Peter 3:10).
>
> And I saw a great white throne, and him that sat on it, from whose face the earth and the heaven fled away; and there was found no place for them (Rev. 20:11).

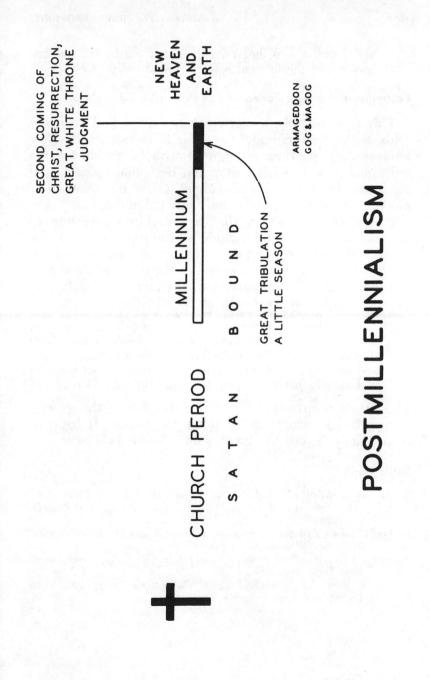

> And I saw a new heaven and a new earth: for the first heaven and the first earth were passed away (Rev. 21:1).

## Postmillennial Interpretation of Revelation 20:1-6

This is exclusively a martyr scene. John had seen the souls of the martyrs under the altar in Revelation 6. Now he sees them on thrones reigning with Christ during the millennial period. Earlier they had been told to wait until all would be avenged and judged (Rev. 6). Now they are present at the time of the great judgment.

Postmillenarians affirm that a literal interpretation of Revelation 20:1-6 would exclude all the righteous from the great white throne judgment. This, they say, cannot be since "the book of *life*" is opened at the great white throne judgment. The first resurrection, therefore, is spiritual in nature; it is the regeneration of the soul into eternal life.

> And you hath he quickened, who were dead in trespasses and sins. . . . Even when we were dead in sins, hath quickened us together with Christ, (by grace ye are saved;) and hath raised us up together, and made us sit together in heavenly places in Christ Jesus (Eph. 2:1, 5, 6).

The second resurrection is of the body. This is the general resurrection in which all the dead participate. It happens immediately before the great white throne judgment.

## Bibliography

Brown, David. *Christ's Second Coming*. Edinburgh: T. and T. Clark, 1882.

Hodge, A. A. *Outlines of Theology*. Grand Rapids, Michigan: William B. Eerdmans, 1928.

Hodge, Charles. *Systematic Theology*, volumes I and II. Grand Rapids, Michigan: William B. Eerdmans, 1940.

Snowden, James H. *The Coming of the Lord: Will It Be Premillennial?* New York: Macmillan, 1922.

Walvoord, John F. "Postmillennialism," *Bibliotheca Sacra*, 106:149-68 (April, 1949).

# AMILLENNIALISM

## Definition

Amillennialism is a theological position which affirms the second coming of Christ to be after the millennial period. In that sense it is basically postmillennial. The term "amillennialism" means "no millennium." This is a misnomer, in a sense, since amillenarians do believe in a millennium, though not a literal, but a spiritual and heavenly, one.

## Method of Scripture Interpretation

Amillenarians follow three basic principles of interpretation:

1. Spiritualization of the Scripture. For seven arguments advanced in support of this principle, see Floyd Hamilton, *The Basis of Millennial Faith*, pp. 54-57.
2. Old Testament promises to Israel are fulfilled in the Church.
3. The millennium is nowhere found in the Bible except in Revelation 20, which being in a book of signs and symbols, is to be interpreted symbolically.

## Nature of the Millennium and Its Relation to World History

Amillenarians affirm the thousand years to be a figurative expression of the complete present period from the resurrection of Christ to His second coming. During this time

Christ is reigning on His throne in a spiritual kingdom
with the disembodied spirits in heaven.

> Verily I say unto you, There be some standing here, which
> shall not taste of death, till they see the Son of man coming
> in his kingdom (Matt. 16:28).

> Therefore being a prophet, and knowing that God had
> sworn with an oath to him, that of the fruit of his loins,
> according to the flesh, he would raise up Christ to sit on
> his throne. . . . For David is not ascended into the heavens:
> but he saith himself, The Lord said unto my Lord, Sit thou
> on my right hand (Acts 2:30, 34).

Amillenarians interpret the word "souls" in Revelation 20:
4 to refer to the disembodied spirits of men in heaven.
They cite as evidence the 100 times (out of 105) in the
New Testament that this word unquestionably refers to
disembodied spirits. They interpret the first resurrection
(Rev. 20) to be the new birth of the believer. The believer in accepting Christ begins to reign with Him on
earth in a spiritual sense.

> Who hath delivered us from the power of darkness, and
> hath translated us into the kingdom of his dear son (Col.
> 1:13).

> That ye would walk worthy of God, who hath called you
> unto his kingdom and glory (1 Thess. 2:12).

> Wherefore we receiving a kingdom which cannot be moved,
> let us have grace, whereby we may serve God acceptably
> with reverence and godly fear (Heb. 12:28).

> And hath made us kings and priests unto God and his
> Father; to him be glory and dominion for ever and ever . . .
> I, John, who also am your brother, and companion in tribu-
> lation, and in the kingdom and patience of Jesus Christ,
> was in the isle that is called Patmos (Rev. 1:6, 9).

At death the believer continues to reign with Christ during
this present age as a disembodied spirit in heaven.

> To him that overcometh will I grant to sit with me in my
> throne, even as I also overcame, and am set down with
> my Father in his throne (Rev. 3:21).

> And I saw thrones, and they sat upon them, and judgment was given unto them: and I saw the souls of them that were beheaded for the witness of Jesus, and for the word of God, and which had not worshipped the beast, neither his image, neither had received his mark upon their foreheads, or in their hands; and they lived and reigned with Christ a thousand years (Rev. 20:4).

1. Nature of the kingdom.

The kingdom is spiritual and heavenly, not political and earthly.

    a. Repentance and the new birth are necessary for entrance into this spiritual kingdom.

> Repent ye: for the kingdom of heaven is at hand (Matt. 3:2).

> The time is fulfilled, and the kingdom of God is at hand: repent ye, and believe the gospel (Mark 1:15).

> Except a man be born again, he cannot see the kingdom of God . . . Except a man be born of the water and of the Spirit, he cannot enter into the kingdom of God (John 3: 3, 5).

    b. Forgiveness, meekness, humility, unselfishness, etc., characterize the kingdom. (Sermon of the Mount)

    c. Christ's kingdom is in heaven, not in the earthly Jerusalem. Christ said to Peter that His kingdom is not of this world (John 18:36). Christ also refused every effort of the Jews to make Him King (John 6:15). Instead He encouraged allegiance to Caesar. He never sought to overthrow the Roman rule (Matt. 22:21).

    d. Kingdom prophecies of the Old Testament given to Israel are fulfilled in the Church as the true Israel, since national birth for an Israelite does not guarantee spiritual blessings.

> They are not all Israel, which are of Israel; Neither, because they are the seed of Abraham, are they all children: but, in Isaac shall thy seed be called. That is, they which are the children of the flesh, these are not the children of

God; but the children of the promise are counted for the seed (Rom. 9:6-8).

For he is not a Jew, which is one outwardly; neither is that circumcision, which is outward in the flesh: But he is a Jew, which is one inwardly; and circumcision is that of the heart, in the spirit, and not in the letter (Rom. 2:28, 29).

Know ye therefore that they which are of faith, the same are the children of Abraham. . . . There is neither bond nor free, there is neither male nor female: for ye are all one in Christ Jesus. And if ye be Christ's, then are ye Abraham's seed, and heirs according to the promise (Gal. 3:7, 28, 29).

For we are the circumcision, which worship God in the spirit, and rejoice in Christ Jesus, and have no confidence in the flesh (Phil. 3:3).

2. Establishment of the kingdom.

The kingdom began at Christ's first coming, since Christ said that the kingdom was already present in His time.

And from the days of John the Baptist until now the kingdom of heaven suffereth violence, and the violent take it by force. For all the prophets and the law prophesied until John (Matt. 11:12, 13).

Neither shall they say, Lo here! or, lo there! for, behold, the kingdom of God is within you (Luke 17:21).

The kingdom is present and universal, established in the hearts of believers (Matt. 11:12; Luke 17:21).

a. Jesus and John the Baptist announced the kingdom as "at hand."

The law and the prophets were until John: since that time the kingdom of God is preached, and every man presseth into it (Luke 16:16).

b. Jesus announced a world-wide kingdom (John 1:19 - 4:45).

For God so loved the world, that he gave his only begotten Son, that whosoever believeth in him should not perish, but have everlasting life (John 3:16).

| Old Testament Promise of . . . | Fulfilled . . . |
| --- | --- |
| David's throne being established forever, not after the manner of men (2 Sam. 7: 16, 19; Isa. 9:6, 7). | When Christ ascended to heaven to the right hand of God (Acts 2:29-36). No temporal kingdom can be eternal. |
| Jerusalem as capital of the kingdom (Isa. 2:3). | In spiritual Zion, the church militant (Heb. 12:22, 23; Gal. 4:26). |
| Restoration of Israel to Palestine (Jer. 23:6-8; Ezek. 37: 1-12). | In a better and heavenly country (Heb. 11:10, 14-16). |
| Time of peace and rest from enemies when Israel shall possess the nations (Isa. 2: 4; Micah 4:1, 2). | In grafting of Gentiles, wild olive branch (Rom. 11:11, 17) into Israel, tame olive tree (Acts 15:17). |
| Restoration of nature (Isa. 11:5-9). | Heaven described under earthly terms. |
| Restoration of temple worship (Ezek. 40 - 48). | One of the following: 1. "a figurative representation and type of the gracious presence of the Lord in His Church . . . which will manifest itself when our Lord shall appear." (Carl F. Keil) 2. The rebuilt temple of restoration days with some elements referring to the new heaven and the new earth. (Martin Wyngaarden) 3. As a symbol of the manifestation of the kingdom of God on earth in government, church, and civilization as God meant them to be. (Floyd Hamilton) |

c. The kingdom was offered to Gentiles as well as to Jews.

The land of Zabulon, and the land of Nephthalim, by the way of the sea, beyond Jordan, Galilee of the Gentiles; the people which sat in darkness saw great light; and to them which sat in the region and shadow of death light is sprung up. From that time Jesus began to preach, and to say, Repent: for the kingdom of heaven is at hand (Matt. 4:15-17).

For mine eyes have seen thy salvation, which thou hast prepared before the face of all people; a light to lighten the Gentiles, and the glory of thy people Israel (Luke 2: 30-32).

## 3. Growth and final form of the kingdom.

Amillenarians interpret the parable of wheat and tares as describing the condition of the kingdom in the world during this present age. Good and evil, represented by the wheat and tares, will grow together until the judgment. The tares are the unbelieving children of the devil; the wheat is the invisible believing church, or members of His spiritual kingdom. Evil will grow progressively worse, violating and persecuting the good. At the end of this present age evil will climax in a super political, economic, and religious force under the Antichrist who will persecute and kill great numbers of believers in a time of great tribulation.

At the second coming of Christ the wicked will be gathered "out of the kingdom." Then "shall the righteous shine forth as the sun in the kingdom of their Father," that is, in the eternal kingdom of God (Matt. 13:14).

### Relation of the Millennium to the Binding of Satan

Since the millennium of Revelation 20 describes the present period between the first and second comings of Christ, it follows that Satan's binding takes place during this present age.

> But when the Pharisees heard it, they said, This fellow doth not cast out devils, but by Beelzebub the prince of the devils. And Jesus knew their thoughts, and said unto them, Every kingdom divided against itself is brought to desolation; and every city or house divided against itself shall not stand: And if Satan cast out Satan, he is divided against himself, how shall then his kingdom stand? And if I by Beelzebub cast out devils, by whom do your children cast them out? therefore they shall be your judges. But if I cast out devils by the Spirit of God, then the kingdom of God is come unto you. Or else how can one enter into a strong man's house, and spoil his goods, except he first bind the strong man? and then he will spoil his house (Matt. 12: 24-29).

> Now is the judgment of this world: now shall the prince of this world be cast out (John 12:31).

> And having spoiled principalities and powers, he made a shew of them openly, triumphing over them in it (Col. 2: 15).

> Forasmuch then as the children are partakers of flesh and blood, he also himself likewise took part of the same; that through death he might destroy him that had the power of death, that is, the devil (Heb. 2:14).

Christ bound Satan: (1) by resisting him in the wilderness; (2) by paying the penalty of sin to redeem man; (3) by destroying the power of death in His resurrection; and (4) by particularly offering salvation to the Gentiles, making it impossible for Satan to deceive the nations any more.

> And cast him into the bottomless pit, and shut him up, and set a seal upon him, that he should deceive the nations no more, till the thousand years should be fulfilled (Rev. 20: 3).

Though Satan can still deceive individuals, no longer can he deceive nations.

> Be sober, be vigilant; because your adversary, the devil, as a roaring lion, walketh about, seeking whom he may devour (1 Peter 5:8).

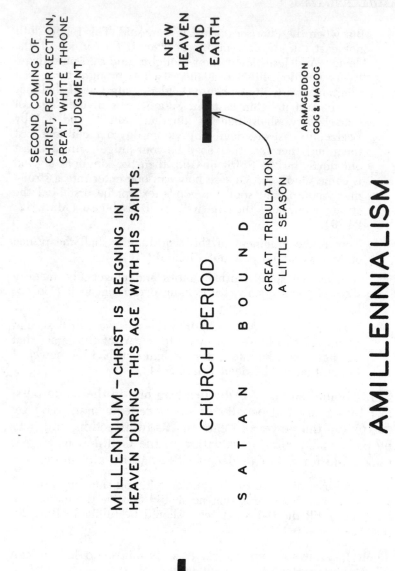

SECOND COMING OF
CHRIST, RESURRECTION,
GREAT WHITE THRONE
JUDGMENT

NEW
HEAVEN
AND
EARTH

ARMAGEDDON
GOG & MAGOG

MILLENNIUM — CHRIST IS REIGNING IN
HEAVEN DURING THIS AGE WITH HIS SAINTS.

CHURCH PERIOD

S A T A N   B O U N D

GREAT TRIBULATION
A LITTLE SEASON

AMILLENNIALISM

## Relation of the Millennium to the Jews

Amillenarians affirm that the Jews have been promised no future *earthly* kingdom. They will be saved only within the Church during this present age, or they will be saved when Christ returns as they look on Him whom they have pierced.

## Relation of the Millennium to the Great Tribulation

Immediately preceding the second coming of Christ, Satan will be loosed for a little season to deceive the nations once again. Satan will cause the preaching of the Gospel to cease and will persuade the nations to believe a lie. He will gather the nations under Antichrist to war against the saints. When Satan and his hosts arrive almost at the point of victory in the battle of Armageddon, Christ will come the second time to judge the earth and Satan, destroying the Antichrist at His appearance.

> And when the thousand years are expired, Satan shall be loosed out of his prison, and shall go out to deceive the nations . . . to gather them together to battle . . . and they went up on the breadth of the earth, and compassed the camp of the saints about, and the beloved city: and fire came down from God out of heaven and devoured them. . . . (Rev. 20:7-9; cf. Rev. 19:11-18; 16:16)

## Relation of the Millennium to the Second Coming, Resurrection, Judgment, and Final Consummation

Amillenarians hold that at the close of the thousand years of Revelation 20, that is, at the end of this present age, Christ will return to earth. There will be a general resurrection of all the dead.

> Marvel not at this: for the hour is coming, in the which all that are in the graves shall hear his voice, and shall come forth; they that have done good, unto the resurrection of life; and they that have done evil, unto the resurrection of damnation (John 5:28, 29).

And have hope toward God, which they themselves also allow, that there shall be a resurrection of the dead, both of the just and unjust (Acts 24:15).

And at that time shall Michael stand up, the great prince which standeth for the children of thy people: and there shall be a time of trouble, such as never was since there was a nation even to that same time: and at that time thy people shall be delivered, every one that shall be found written in the book. And many of them that sleep in the dust of the earth shall awake, some to everlasting life, and some to shame and everlasting contempt (Dan. 12:1, 2).

The living saints will be transfigured and raptured to meet the Lord in the air.

Then shall two be in the field; the one shall be taken, and the other left. Two women shall be grinding at the mill; the one shall be taken, and the other left (Matt. 24:40, 41).

. . . the dead in Christ shall rise first: then we which are alive and remain shall be caught up together with them in the clouds, to meet the Lord in the air: and so shall we ever be with the Lord (1 Thess. 4:13-17).

After the rapture Christ and His Church either return to earth or remain in heaven for the judgment of the great white throne. The wicked will be judged and consigned to everlasting punishment.

Then shall the King say unto them on his right hand, Come, ye blessed of my Father, inherit the kingdom prepared for you from the foundation of the world. . . . Then shall he say also unto them on the left hand, Depart from me, ye cursed, into everlasting fire, prepared for the devil and his angels: . . . And these shall go away into everlasting punishment: but the righteous into life eternal (Matt. 25:34, 41, 46).

The old heaven and the old earth will pass away, and the eternal kingdom of God will be established in a new heaven and on a new earth, which will be characterized by righteousness, and God shall be all and in all (1 Cor. 15: 24-28).

## Amillennial Interpretation of Revelation 20

Amillenarians assert this passage to describe the souls of the saints in heaven between the first and second coming of Christ. The "first resurrection" is the new birth of the believer. The other resurrection is the general bodily resurrection at Christ's return. Believers begin to reign with Christ at the time of their regeneration in a spiritual sense.

> Who hath delivered us from the power of darkness, and hath translated us into the kingdom of his dear Son (Col. 1:13).

> That ye would walk worthy of God, who hath called you unto his kingdom and glory (1 Thess. 2:12).

> Wherefore we receiving a kingdom which cannot be moved, let us have grace, whereby we may serve God acceptably with reverence and godly fear (Heb. 12:28).

Believers continue to reign with Christ at their death as disembodied spirits in heaven.

> To him that overcometh will I grant to sit with me in my throne, even as I also overcame, and am set down with my Father in his throne (Rev. 3:21).

> And I saw thrones, and they sat upon them, and judgment was given unto them, and I saw the souls of them that were beheaded for the witness of Jesus, and for the word of God, and which had not worshipped the beast, neither his image, neither had received his mark upon their foreheads, or in their hands; and they lived and reigned with Christ a thousand years (Rev. 20:4).

## Bibliography

Allis, Oswald T. *Prophecy and the Church*. Philadelphia: Presbyterian and Reformed Publishing Company, 1945.

Berkhof, Louis. *Systematic Theology*. Grand Rapids, Michigan: William B. Eerdmans, 1946.

Hamilton, Floyd E. *The Basis of Millennial Faith*. Grand Rapids, Michigan: William B. Eerdmans, 1948.

Masselink, William. *Why Thousand Years?* Grand Rapids, Michigan: William B. Eerdmans, 1930.

Murray, George L. *Millennial Studies*. Grand Rapids, Michigan: Baker Book House, 1948.

Payne, Homer Lemuel. "Contemporary Amillennial Literature." *Bibliotheca Sacra*, 106:200-10 (April, 1949); 106:342-45 (July, 1949); 106:486-92 (October, 1949); 107:103-10 (January, 1950)

Pieters, Albertus. *The Seed of Abraham*. Grand Rapids, Michigan: William B. Eerdmans, 1950.

Reid, R. J. *Remarks on the Amillennialism and Kindred Teachings of Philip Mauro*, New York: Loizeaux Brothers, 1943.

Terry, Milton S. *Biblical Hermeneutics*. Grand Rapids, Michigan: Zondervan Publishing House, 1911.

Vos, Gerhardus. *Biblical Theology*. Grand Rapids, Michigan: William B. Eerdmans, 1948.

————. *The Pauline Eschatology*. Princeton, New Jersey: Princeton University Press, 1930.

Walvoord, John F. "Amillennialism," *Bibliotheca Sacra*, 106:291-302 (July, 1949); 106:420-32 (October, 1949); 107:42-50 (January, 1950); 107:154-67 (April, 1950); 107:281-90 (July, 1950); 107:420-29 (October, 1950); 108:7-14 (January, 1951).

Wyngaarden, Martin. *The Future of the Kingdom in Prophecy and Fulfillment*. Grand Rapids, Michigan: Zondervan Publishing House, 1934.

Young, Edward J. *The Prophecy of Daniel*. Grand Rapids, Michigan: William B. Eerdmans, 1949.

# PREMILLENNIALISM

## Definition

Premillenarians hold that Christ's second coming precedes His establishment of a glorious kingdom of peace and righteousness on earth. He shall personally reign from Jerusalem with His saints.

## Method of Interpretation

Premillenarians hold to the grammatical, historical, and literal·interpretation of Scripture, wherever possible. The Old Testament prophecies concerning the restoration and future glory of Israel and the establishment of a Messianic kingdom on earth are to be literally fulfilled. Martin Luther said, "The literal sense of Scripture alone is the whole essence of faith and of Christian theology." (Farrar)

## Nature of the Millennium, Final Form of the Kingdom, and Its Relation to World History

Premillenarians hold the thousand years to be the duration of a personal reign of Christ from Jerusalem over the nations of the world immediately following His second coming. The prophecies in the Old and the New Testaments concerning the Messianic Kingdom are interpreted as finding their fulfillment in this future millennial kingdom.

115

## 1. *Nature of this Messianic kingdom*

### a. A universal theocracy

Christ Himself shall rule as King over all the nations of
the earth. Jerusalem, rebuilt, enlarged, and adorned, will
be the capital. The prophecy given to David that his kingdom would be established *forever* is interpreted as referring
to Christ's kingdom, since Christ is of the lineage of David
(2 Sam. 7:16).

> Once have I sworn by my holiness that I will not lie unto
> David. His seed shall endure for ever, and his throne as
> the sun before me. It shall be established for ever as the
> moon, and as a faithful witness in heaven (Ps. 89:35-37;
> cf. 110:1, 2; Isa. 55:3-5; Acts 2:29-31).

### b. An era of universal peace and righteousness to all nations

> And he shall judge among the nations, and shall rebuke
> many people: and they shall beat their swords into plow-
> shares, and their spears into pruninghooks: nation shall not
> lift up sword against nation, neither shall they learn war
> any more (Isa. 2:4; cf. 66:12; Micah 4:3-5; Zech. 9:10; Isa.
> 2:4; Ps. 85:8; Hab. 2:14).

### c. The restoration of all nature.

There will be peace between man and beast and between
beast and beast. Palestine will blossom as a rose.

> The wolf also shall dwell with the lamb, and the leopard
> shall lie down with the kid; and the calf and the young
> lion and the fatling together; and a little child shall lead
> them. . . . And the sucking child . . . shall put his hand
> on the cockatrice's den. They shall not hurt nor destroy in
> all my holy mountain: for the earth shall be full of the
> knowledge of the Lord, as the waters cover the sea (Isa.
> 11:6-9).

> The wilderness and the solitary place shall be glad for
> them; and the desert shall rejoice, and blossom as the rose.
> It shall blossom abundantly and rejoice even with joy and

singing. . . . And the parched ground shall become a pool, and the thirsty land springs of water. . . (Isa. 35:1-10).

Behold, the days come, saith the Lord, that the plowman shall overtake the reaper, and the treader of grapes him that soweth seed; and the mountains shall drop sweet wine, and all the hills shall melt. And I will bring again the captivity of my people of Israel, and they shall build the waste cities, and inhabit them. . . . And I will plant them upon their land, and they shall no more be pulled up out of their land which I have given them, saith the Lord thy God (Amos 9:13-15).

d. Christianity will be the universal religion: all false systems and idols will be destroyed.

Look unto me, and be ye saved, all the ends of the earth: for I am God, and there is none else. I have sworn by myself, and the word is gone out of my mouth in righteousness, and shall not return. That unto me every knee shall bow, every tongue shall swear . . . (Isa. 45:22-25).

And it shall come to pass in that day, saith the Lord of hosts, that I will cut off the names of the idols out of the land, and they shall no more be remembered: and also I will cause the prophets and the unclean spirits to pass out of the land (Zech. 13:2).

e. Longevity will characterize the people living during the millennium.

There will be no deaths except of the wicked and unbelieving.

There shall be no more thence an infant of days, nor an old man that hath not filled his days: for the child shall die an hundred years old, but the sinner being an hundred years old shall be accursed (Isa. 65:20; cf. 65:17-19, 21-23).

## 2. *Establishment, growth, and final form of the kingdom*

Premillenarians affirm that since the Old Testament prophecies have not as yet been fulfilled, their literal fulfillment must of necessity be future. Daniel prophesied the

establishment of this kingdom after the kingdoms of the
earth are destroyed (Dan. 2:44; 7:26, 27). Concerning the
kingdom, Christ taught in the parable of the pounds that
He would return "having received the kingdom" (Luke 19:
15). This cannot refer to the end of the world, for at that
time Christ will deliver up the kingdom of God the Father
(1 Cor. 15:24). Hence, these passages teach that the kingdom must be established between Christ's second coming
and the "end" when He delivers up the kingdom to God
the Father. This is the clear teaching also of Revelation 20
when interpreted literally.

This millennial kingdom was not established at Christ's
first coming:

1. It was not established in Christ's day.

   a. Joseph of Arimathea understood it to be future; he
      was "waiting for the kingdom of God" (Mark 15:43).

   b. The thief on the cross understood it to be future,
      and was not corrected for any error by Christ: "Re-
      member me when thou comest into thy kingdom,"
      he said to Christ on the cross (Luke 23:42).

   c. Christ taught the disciples to pray for the kingdom
      to come (Matt. 6:10).

2. The Apostle Paul looked to the future for its fulfillment:
"Who shall judge the quick and the dead at his appearing
and his kingdom" (2 Tim. 4:1).

3. The New Testament elsewhere also teaches the establishment of the kingdom to be at Christ's second coming.

> And the seventh angel sounded; and there were great voices
> in heaven, saying, The kingdoms of this world are become
> the kingdoms of our Lord, and of his Chirst; and he shall
> reign for ever and ever (Rev. 11:15-18).

Many present-day premillenarians hold that a literal Messianic kingdom was offered by Christ at His first coming.

Christ came first to Israel as King. The Jews, however, rejected His kingdom. Whereupon, the kingdom was postponed and held in abeyance until the second coming of
Christ, when it will be realized. For a full discussion, see
KINGDOM).

Some present-day premillenarians hold, however, that
Christ had no intention of setting up an earthly political
kingdom at His first coming, but that He came the first
time to offer salvation to Jew and Gentile alike, and to
become the Lamb of God that takes away the sin of the
world. At His second coming Christ will establish an earthly, political kingdom which will be the material realization
of the Davidic kingdom promised in the Old Testament.
Christ will then reign in His kingdom with those who have
followed Him in regeneration (Matt. 19:28; 2 Tim. 2:12).
Those who hold this view affirm that the Scriptures teach
the following:

a. The present state of the kingdom of God is a state
   of righteousness, peace, and joy in the Holy Spirit
   (Rom. 14:17).

b. John the Baptist, Christ and His disciples at His
   first coming, preached repentance as necessary for
   entrance into the kingdom (Matt. 3:2; John 3:3, 5).

c. This kingdom of salvation was offered to all, being
   proclaimed to Israel first since they were Christ's
   own kindred in the flesh and bearers of the promises
   (Luke 2:30-32; Matt. 10:5-7; John 4:39-42; 10:16;
   Rom. 9:4, 5; 10:11-14; Isa. 49:6).

d. The terms "kingdom of heaven" and "kingdom of
   God" are used interchangeably (Matt. 19:23, 24;
   13:24; 4:17; Mark 1:14).

e. This kingdom will be realized in an earthly, political
   sense at the second coming of Christ (Matt. 25:31;
   Luke 19:12-15; 21:31; 2 Tim. 4:1).

### Relation of the Millennium to Israel and the Church

The Church of the New Testament includes both believing Jews and believing Gentiles. Israel as a nation is never referred to as the Church. The believing Jews and Gentiles of the New Testament are counted as the spiritual seed of Abraham since they have been blessed in Christ as the fulfillment of the promise to Abraham.

> Therefore it is of faith, that it might be by grace; to the end the promise might be sure to all the seed; not to that only which is of the law, but to that also which is of the faith of Abraham; who is the father of us all (Rom. 4:16; cf. Gal. 3:7, 14, 28, 29).

The Church does not, however, absorb in a spiritual manner the national promises also given to Abraham and his seed after the flesh. Abraham's seed after the flesh, Israel as a nation, was never completely cast off by God, in spite of its rejection of the Messiah; but blindness in part has happened to national Israel until the fulness of the Gentiles is come.

> For I would not, brethren, that ye should be ignorant of this mystery, lest ye should be wise in your own conceits; that blindness in part is happened to Israel, until the fulness of the Gentiles be come in (Rom. 11:25).

When Christ comes again, those of the nation Israel who are living at the time will look on Him Whom they have pierced and will be saved.

> And I will pour upon the house of David, and upon the inhabitants of Jerusalem, the spirit of grace and of supplications: and they shall look upon me whom they have pierced, and they shall mourn for him, as one mourneth for his only son, and shall be in bitterness for him, as one that is in bitterness for his firstborn (Zech. 12:10).
>
> And so all Israel shall be saved: as it is written, There shall come out of Sion the Deliverer, and shall turn away ungodliness from Jacob (Rom. 11:26; Isa. 66:8; Jer. 23:5, 6; 33:8; Ezek. 11:19, 20).

The nation Israel will be regathered and restored to the land of Palestine.

> Behold, I will gather them out of all countries, whither I have driven them in mine anger, and in my fury, and in great wrath; and I will bring them again unto this place, and I will cause them to dwell safely . . . for I will cause their captivity to return (Jer. 32:37, 44; cf. Isa. 11:12; Hosea 3:4, 5; Micah 4:6-8).

No longer will it be a divided nation; but Israel and Judah will be reunited as one nation (Isa. 11:13; Jer. 3:18; 50:4). The land of Palestine will be distributed again among the tribes (Ezek. 47:13-23; 48). Israel will be exalted as chief among the nations (Isa. 14:1, 2; 60:1-22; 61:5; 66:12; Zech. 8:23).

Some hold that the converted, restored Jewish nation will govern the world during the millennium; others, that the resurrected saints will be on earth and reign with Christ; others, that the resurrected saints will not be on earth but in heaven during the millennium and govern the world with Christ from heaven; still others, that the resurrected saints who were martyred for their testimony will be those who reign with Christ.

Some affirm that the Church will preach the Gospel in all the world for a witness before the end (Matt. 24:14). They believe that the Church will go through the great tribulation. Others, however, see the 144,000 of the tribes of Israel, Jewish evangelists, as the preachers of the Gospel during the tribulation days (Rev. 7). Those who affirm this latter view believe that the Church will be raptured before the tribulation. (See RAPTURE.)

### Relation of the Millennium to the Binding of Satan

At the beginning of the millennium Satan and his hosts will be bound and cast into the bottomless pit for the thousand years. Satan will no longer deceive the nations (Rev. 20:1-21; cf. Isa. 24:21, 22; 27:1; Rev. 20:1-21).

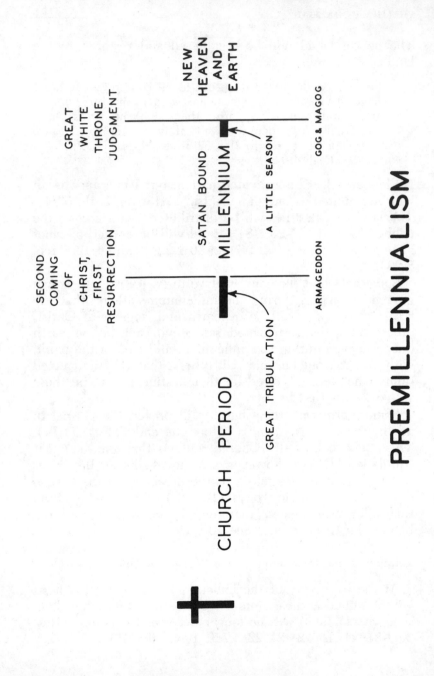

PREMILLENNIALISM

At the end of the thousand years, however, Satan will be loosed for a little season and will deceive the nations once again. He will organize Gog and Magog to besiege the camp of the saints and Jerusalem. Fire will come down out of heaven and destroy them (Rev. 20:7-9). Then Satan will be judged and cast into the lake of fire and brimstone to be tormented day and night forever. The events of Revelation 20 - 21 are to me interpreted as literal and consecutive.

### Relation of the Millennium to the Great Tribulation

Immediately preceding the second coming of Christ, there will be a brief period of great tribulation on earth during the manifestation and reign of the Antichrist. At the close of this period, under the leadership of Antichrist and the false prophet, the kings of the earth will assemble at Armageddon to make war against the Lord. Then Christ will return to earth and destroy them, after which He will set up the millennial kingdom.

> Thou sawest till that a stone was cut out without hands, which smote the image upon his feet that were of iron and clay, and brake them to pieces. Then was the iron, the clay, the brass, the silver, and the gold, broken to pieces together, and became like the chaff of the summer threshing-floors; and the wind carried them away, that no place was found for them: and the stone that smote the image became a great mountain, and filled the whole earth. . . . And in the days of these kings shall the God of heaven set up a kingdom, which shall never be destroyed: and the kingdom shall not be left to other people, but it shall break in pieces and consume all these kingdoms, and it shall stand for ever (Dan. 2:34, 35. 44).

> And out of his mouth goeth a sharp sword, that with it he should smite the nations: and he shall rule them with a rod of iron. . . . And I saw the beast, and the kings of the earth, and their armies, gathered together to make war against him that sat on the horse, and against his army (Rev. 19:15, 19; 16:16).

### Relation of the Millennium to the Second Coming of Christ, the Resurrections, Judgments, and the Final Consummation

When Christ comes to establish the millennial kingdom, the first resurrection will take place, which includes the martyred saints and those over whom "the second death hath no power" (Rev. 20:6). All living believers will be transfigured and raptured to meet the Lord in the air.

> Behold, I shew you a mystery; We shall not all sleep, but we shall all be changed, in a moment, in the twinkling of an eye, at the last trump: for the trumpet shall sound, and the dead shall be raised incorruptible, and we shall be changed (1 Cor. 15:51, 52).

> For the Lord himself shall descend from heaven with a shout, with the voice of the archangel, and with the trump of God: and the dead in Christ shall rise first: then we which are alive and remain shall be caught up together with them in the clouds, to meet the Lord in the air: and so shall we ever be with the Lord (1 Thess. 4:16, 17).

The second resurrection, of the wicked dead, does not occur until after the millennium when they shall be judged at the great white throne.

> But the rest of the dead lived not again until the thousand years were finished. This is the first resurrection . . . and I saw a great white throne, and him that sat on it, from whose face the earth and the heaven fled away; and there was found no place for them. And I saw the dead, small and great, stand before God; and the books were opened: and another book was opened, which is the book of life: and the dead were judged out of those things which were written in the books, according to their works . . . And whosoever was not found written in the book of life was cast into the like of fire (Rev. 20:5, 11-15).

Since believers will act as judges of the twelve tribes of Israel, of the world, and of angels, there seems to be a separate judgment of their works before they themselves become judges (Matt. 19:28; 1 Cor. 6:2, 3).

For we must all appear before the judgment seat of Christ; that every one may receive the things done in his body, according to that he hath done, whether it be good or bad (2 Cor. 3:10).

Every man's work shall be made manifest: for the day shall declare it, because it shall be revealed by fire; and the fire shall try every man's work of what sort it is. If any man's work shall be burned, he shall suffer loss: but he himself shall be saved; yet so as by fire (1 Cor. 3:13, 15).

Believers' rewards will be given at the judgment seat of Christ. The Bible lists the following:

1. An incorruptible crown — to those who strive for the mastery in all things (1 Cor. 9:25).

2. A crown of righteousness — to all those who love the Lord's appearing (2 Tim. 4:8).

3. The crown of life — to the man who endures temptation and to those who are faithful even to death (James 1:12; Rev. 2:10).

4. A crown of glory that fades not away — to the shepherds of the flocks who were examples to their flock (1 Peter 5:4).

At the end of the thousand years a new heaven and a new earth will be established. The old heaven and the old earth will be destroyed by fire (2 Peter 3:10; Rev. 20:11; 21:1). At that time Christ shall deliver up the kingdom to God the Father. Then the Son also will be subject to God, who made Christ ruler, and God will be all in all (1 Cor. 15:24, 28).

## Bibliography

Chafer, Lewis Sperry. *Must We Dismiss the Millennium?* Crescent City, Florida: Biblical Testimony League, 1921.

—————. *Systematic Theology.* Grand Rapids, Michigan: Dunham Publishing House, 1948.

Eerdman, Charles R. *The Return of Christ.* New York: Doran, 1922.

Feinberg, Charles. *Premillennialism or Amillennialism?* Grand Rapids, Michigan: Zondervan Publishing House, 1936.

Gray, James M. *A Textbook on Prophecy.* New York: Fleming H. Revell, 1928.

Huffman, Jaspar A. *The Progressive Unfolding of the Messianic Hope.* New York: George H. Doran Company, 1924.

Ironside, H. A. *The Lamp of Prophecy.* Grand Rapids, Michigan: Zondervan Publishing House, 1940.

Kellogg, S. H. *The Jews,* second edition. New York: Anson D. F. Randolph, 1887.

———. "Premillennialism: Its Relation to Doctrine and Practice," *Bibliotheca Sacra,* 99:235-44 (April, 1942); 99:364-72 (July, 1942); 99:486-99 (October, 1942); 100:301-08 (April, 1943).

Ottman, Ford C. *Imperialism and Christ.* New York: Publications Office of *Our Hope,* 1912.

———. *The Unfolding of the Ages.* New York: Baker and Taylor, 1915.

Peters, George N. H. *The Theocratic Kingdom of our Lord Jesus, The Christ.* New York: Funk and Wagnalls, 1884.

Reese, Alexander. *The Approaching Advent of Christ.* London: Marshall, Morgan and Scott, no date.

Riley, William B. *The Evolution of the Kingdom.* Chicago: Charles C. Cook, 1913.

Rutgers, William H. *Premillennialism in America.* Oosterbaan, Holland: Goes, 1930.

Scofield, C. I. *What Do the Prophets Say?* Philadelphia: Sunday School Times Company, 1916.

Walvoord, John F. "Premillennialism," *Bibliotheca Sacra,* 106:153-66 (April, 1951); 106:270-81 (July, 1951); 106:414-22 (October, 1951).

———. "Premillennialism and the Abrahamic Covenant," *Bibliotheca Sacra,* 109:37-46 (January, 1952); 109:136-60 (April, 1952); 109:217-25 (July, 1952); 109:283-303 (October, 1952).

# HISTORY OF MILLENNIALISM

Probably the earliest information of millennialism is from Barnabas, whose writings give evidence of its teachings in his day (A.D. 96). Barnabas himself taught that God would consummate His work in the earth in 6000 years, and then Christ would come and "abolish the season of the wicked one." Since his teaching is not completely given, some have classed him as an amillenarian because he found the promises of Israel fulfilled in the Christian Church.

Justin Martyr (A.D. 100-165), however, had definite premillennial views, appearing chiefly in his "Dialogue with Trypho, a Jew." Trypho asked him: ". . . do you really admit that this place, Jerusalem, shall be rebuilt, and do you expect your people to be gathered together and made joyful with Christ and the patriarchs and the prophets, both the men of our nation and other proselytes who joined them before your Christ came?" Justin answered him, ". . . I and others are of this opinion and believe that such will take place, as you assuredly are aware, but, on the other hand, I signified to you that many who belong to the pure and pious faith and are true Christians think otherwise. But," he concluded, "I and others who are rightminded Christians on all points, are assured that there will be a resurrection of the dead and a thousand years in Jerusalem, which will then be built, adorned, and enlarged, as the prophets Ezekiel and Isaiah and others declare." (D. H. Kromminga, *The Millennium in the Church*).

Irenaeus (A.D. 140-203), the disciple of Polycarp, the disciple of John, was likewise a premillenarian. He spoke of the "times of the kingdom" when the "righteous shall bear rule upon their rising from the dead; when also, the creation, having been renovated and set free, shall fructify with an abundance of all kinds of food, from the dew of the heaven and from the fertility of the earth." (McClintock and Strong).

From Irenaeus also we learn of Papias (A.D. 180-155) as a premillenarian. Papias was reputed to have heard John the disciple. Thus he would become our chief link with the views of the Twelve themselves. Irenaeus said that the tradition that Papias passed along was that the Lord in His day taught concerning the millennium that "vines shall grow, each having 10,000 twigs, and in each one of the shoots, 10,000 clusters and on each one of the clusters, 10,000 grapes, and every grape when pressed will give five and twenty metretes of wine . . ."

Origen (A.D. 180-254) was perhaps the first to allegorize the passages on which the teaching of the millennium was based. His principle of allegorizing Scripture opened the door for a spiritual millennium and the school of amillennialism.

About the middle of the second century there arose an ascetic sect among the Christians, the Montanists. They gathered together in a village of Phrygia, which they named the New Jerusalem, proclaiming thus the establishment of the millennium. There they waited for the Lord's return.

At the end of the second century there was a decline of the doctrine of millennialism. This perhaps was due to: (1) the death of the last of the leaders of Montanism; (2) Christ's return had not occurred; and (3) the excessive descriptions of the millennium handed down from Papias.

During this period, however, there were others who definitely mentioned the millennium in their writings: Nepos of Egypt (first half of the third century), an opponent of Origin, a premillenarian; Methodius (d. A.D. 311), also an opponent of Origen, seems to speak of two resurrections, though his millennialism is not clear; Victorinus (d. A.D. 304), a premillenarian; Lactantius (A.D. 260-330), a premillenarian; and Apollinaris (c. A.D. 382), a premillenarian.

Up to this point in history premillennialism was the prevailing opinion of the church. But with the coming of Augustine (A.D. 354-400), the history of the doctrine took a swing to the left. Augustine claimed to be premillenarian, but changed to become an amillenarian. He said that he did not find the doctrine of the premillenarians objectionable, provided that the joys of the righteous were figurative. He spiritualized the millennium, finding its fulfillment in the church. The millennial reign of the saints was heavenly between the first and second comings of Christ, which period would end in and around A.D. 1000. The first resurrection was the new birth. "The church now on earth is both the kingdom of Christ and the kingdom of heaven. . . , the saints being with Him now. Thrones (Rev. 20) may not be understood of the last judgment, but by the thrones are meant the ruler's places in the church, and the persons themselves by whom it is governed. . . . The church which is now is the kingdom of God. Thus then, the church reigns with Christ. . . . Christ's kingdom is the church" (Augustine, *The City of God*, as quoted in *Ante-Nicene Fathers*, Volume 2, p. 256). It is clear that the seeds of modern amillennialism were heavily sown by Augustine. Sometimes he is called the "father of amillennialism."

During the Middle Ages, the church continued its adherence to Augustine's view, more or less modified when Christ failed to return at Augustine's predicted time of His return at A.D. 1000. With the cessation of persecution the conviction that the Gospel could probably win the world found a place in the church. Hence, the millenarians of this period were of the postmillennial type. Hildegard and Joachim of Floris (A.D. 1130-1202) were perhaps the best known. Joachim innovated what is called sometimes a Trinitarian Millennialism. The Old Testament was the age of the Father; the New Testament was the age of the Son; and the age of the Holy Spirit will be millennium, after which Christ would return.

In Reformation days the doctrine of a millennium was branded as heresy by Luther (A.D. 1483-1546). The idea of a millennium was rejected as a Jewish opinion by the Augsburg Confession and by the Helvetic Confession. The Augsburg Confession reads: "They condemn others also, who now scatter abroad Jewish opinions, that, before the resurrection of the dead the godly shall occupy the kingdoms of the world, the wicked being everywhere oppressed" (Schaff, *Creeds of Christendom,* Article XVII). The Helvetic Confession reads: "We reject all who deny the real resurrection. . . . We also reject the Jewish dream of a millennium, or golden age on earth, before the last judgment." *(Ibid.,* Article XI)

Calvin (A.D. 1509-1564) said that the teaching of millennialism was "fiction too puerile to need or deserve refutation" (Calvin's *Institutes of Religion).*

A summary of ancient millennialism — or chiliasm as it was called then — reveals a dominant premillennial note. That of the Middle Ages reveals predominantly a postmillennial note. Naturally, succeeding generations fell heir to the crystallized thought of both schools of thought. In the Reformation days a group of people known as the Anabaptists held a combination of both views. English Congregationalists adopted the postmillenarian position. Premillennialism had some adherents among the Lutheran theologians, some of whom were Philip Jacob Spener (1634-1705), Johannes Cocceius (1603-1669), and John Albecht Bengel (1687-1751). Bengel had the misfortune of setting the date of Christ's return at 1846. Van Oosterzee was also premillenarian. He considered the thousand years of the millennium to be symbolical of a longer period, however. (For a list of nineteenth century premillenarians, see Reese, *The Approaching Advent of Christ,* p. 18.)

In the last three centuries many sects have also held to various features of the premillennial return of Christ: the Irvingites; Second Adventists (disciples of William Miller, 1831 on); Mormonism (or Latter Day Saints, followers of Joseph Smith); Jehovah Witnesses (followers of Russel and Rutherford).

More recent writers of millennialism are listed under the particular view that they represent as above.

# RAPTURE

The word "rapture" does not itself appear in the Scriptures; it has been applied to the doctrine of the "catching away" or transporting of believers from the earth to heaven by the Lord at His second coming. The word is derived from the Latin verb, *rapere,* "to seize," hence, "to transport."

The doctrine of the rapture is almost universally held. There are, however, varying views as to the time when this event will take place. These views may be divided into three groups:

1. Those who believe the rapture to take place *before* the time of the great tribulation of the earth (Pre-tribulation rapture).

2. Those who believe the rapture to take place sometime *during* the tribulation period (Mid-tribulation rapture). This view distinguishes itself from the first view in that the last half of the tribulation period is held to be extremely severe and tense. It is usually spoken of as being "the great tribulation."

3. Those who hold that the rapture will take place *after* the tribulation period (Post-tribulation rapture).

A diagram, a summary of the arguments of each of the views, and a bibliography of recent writers of those holding these respective interpretations are as follows:

# PRE-TRIBULATION RAPTURE

Those who affirm this position usually divide the second coming of Christ into two phases. Christ will come *for* His saints (the rapture, the parousia, or presence); afterwards, He will come *with* His saints (the revelation, epiphany, or appearing of Christ).

> But I would not have you to be ignorant, brethren, concerning them which are asleep, that ye sorrow not, even as others which have no hope. For if we believe that Jesus died and rose again, even so them also which sleep in Jesus will God bring with him. For this we say unto you by the word of the Lord, that we which are alive and remain unto the coming of the Lord shall not prevent them which are asleep. For the Lord himself shall descend from heaven with a shout, with the voice of the archangel, and with the trump of God: and the dead in Christ shall rise first: Then we which are alive and remain shall be caught up together with them in the clouds, to meet the Lord in the air: and so shall we ever be with the Lord (1 Thess. 4:13-17).

> Behold, the Lord cometh with ten thousands of his saints (Jude 14).

> And I saw heaven opened, and behold a white horse; and he that sat upon him was called Faithful and True, and in righteousness he doth judge and make war. . . . And the armies which were in heaven followed him upon white horses, clothed in fine linen, white and clean (Rev. 19: 11-14).

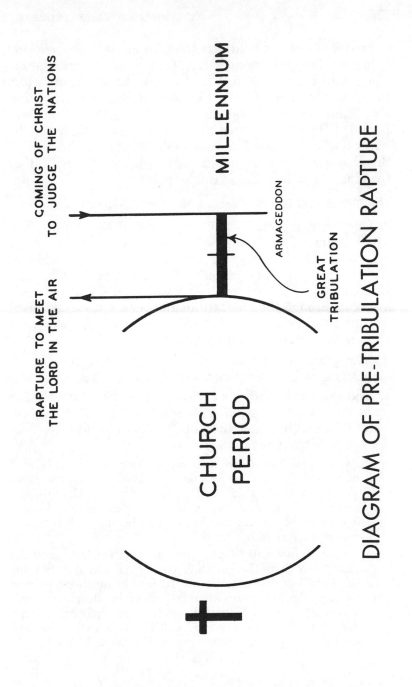

RAPTURE TO MEET THE LORD IN THE AIR

COMING OF CHRIST TO JUDGE THE NATIONS

MILLENNIUM

CHURCH PERIOD

ARMAGEDDON

GREAT TRIBULATION

DIAGRAM OF PRE-TRIBULATION RAPTURE

Pre-tribulationists hold that the Church or those believers living at the time immediately preceding the tribulation, along with those dead in Christ, are to be raptured before the tribulation period. The following reasons are given that the Church will not be on earth during the tribulation period. These arguments have been gleaned from the writers who are listed in the bibliography at the end of the chapter. The evidence is held to be cumulative rather than as dependent on a single point.

### The Church Will Not Go Through the Great Tribulation

Thirty-one arguments for the pre-tribulation rapture are listed below. These can be classified under three major categories: (A) The great tribulation is the punishment of the Christ-rejecting nation of Israel, not of the Christian Church; (B) The nature of the Christian Church forbids its going through the great tribulation; and (C) An interval of time is necessary between Christ's coming *for* and *with* His saints — the Christian Church.

A. *The great tribulation is the punishment of the Christ-rejecting nation of Israel, not of the Christian Church.*

1. The great tribulation is a visitation of the wrath of God upon those who dwell on the earth and on Israel who rejected Christ. It is the time of "Jacob's trouble." It does not concern the Church.

> Ask ye now, and see whether a man doth travail with child? wherefore do I see every man with his hands on his loins, as a woman in travail, and all faces are turned into paleness? Alas! for that day is great, so that none is like it: it is even the time of Jacob's trouble; but he shall be saved out of it (Jer. 30:6, 7).

> And it shall come to pass, that in all the land, saith the Lord, two parts therein shall be cut off and die; but the third shall be left therein. And I will bring the third part through the fire, and will refine them as silver is refined, and will try then as gold is tried: they shall call on my name, and I will hear them: I will say, It is my people: and they shall say, The Lord is my God (Zech. 13:8, 9).

Because thou hast kept the word of my patience, I also will keep thee from the hour of temptation, which shall come upon all the world, to try them that dwell upon the earth (Rev. 3:10). (The word "earthdwellers" is held to have the idea of permanence, and thus to signify those who seek to make earth their permanent dwelling place.)

2. The Scriptures dealing with the tribulation have particular reference to the Jews. The sections in Matthew 24 and Mark 13 which relate to the tribulation and Christ's second coming were spoken to the disciples not as representatives of the Church, but as representatives of the Jewish nation (Matt. 24:1-31; Mark 13:14).

   a. The setting is in Judea.
   b. They were to pray that their flight be not on the Sabbath. Christians do not celebrate the Sabbath.
   c. The abomination is set up, which was prophesied by Daniel as concerning the Jews.
   d. The appearance of the word "elect" must, therefore, refer to the Jews here, and not the Church which is also sometimes so called.

Luke 21:36 is interpreted also as referring to the disciples as representatives of the Jews.

   a. That the section is Jewish is evident from the expressions:
      "this generation" (v. 32)
      "great distress in the land" (v. 23)
      "Jerusalem trodden down" (v. 24)
      "your redemption" (v. 28)
      "kingdom of God nigh at hand" (v. 31)
   b. The Church is not mentioned.
   c. Christ is never called Son of man in relation to the Church and His coming again.
   d. The believers do not stand before Him; they sit on thrones with Him.

3. The tribulation is characterized by gross darkness when there will not be one who has faith. The situation is not true of the faithful Church.

For, behold, the darkness shall cover the earth, and gross darkness the people: but the Lord shall arise upon thee, and his glory shall be seen upon thee (Isa. 60:2; cf. Jer. 13:16).

Nevertheless when the Son of man cometh, shall he find faith on the earth? (Luke 18:8)

Who hath delivered us from the power of darkness, and hath translated us into the kingdom of his dear Son (Col. 1:13; cf. I Peter 2:9; Zech. 12:10 - 13:1; Eph. 5:8).

4. Satan persecutes the woman (Israel) during the tribulation (Rev. 12). The Church must be removed, otherwise, the Church, being the very body of Christ, would be more likely to be persecuted than Israel.

B. *The nature of the Christian Church forbids its going through the great tribulation.*

1. The nature and character of the Church forbids her going into the tribulation, since the tribulation is a day of judgment upon the Christ-rejecting world, both Jewish and Gentile, but more particularly a day of judgment on Israel. The Church is a heavenly people with a heavenly calling and destiny. Israel is an earthly people, with promise of earthly destiny and inheritance (Deut. 28:1-14).

    a. The Church was chosen before the foundation of the world (Eph. 1:4).

    b. The Church is not of the world (John 17:14; Phil. 3:20).

    c. The Church is raised with Christ to sit in the heavenlies (Eph. 1:3; 2:6).

    d. The Church is foreordained to be conformed to the image of Christ (Rom. 8:29).

Those who hold the pre-tribulation view also distinguish between the coming of Christ *for* His Church (John 14: 1, 2) and the coming of the Son of man *with* the angels in glory (Matt. 25:31). The passage in John states that Christ will come in person to receive the Church to Himself; the passage in Matthew indicates that He commissions angels to escort the Church. When Christ comes *for* His Church, He will come alone, just as He ascended alone into heaven. That Christ comes alone for the Church is evident also from 1 Thessalonians 4:16, 17: "The Lord Himself shall descend. . . ."

2. The glorification of the Church requires a resurrection previous to the manifestation of the wrath of the Lamb in Revelation 6:17.

> And that he might make known the riches of his glory on the vessels of mercy, which he had afore prepared unto glory (Rom 9:23).
>
> For the great day of his wrath is come; and who shall be able to stand? (Rev. 6:17)

3. The Church is promised deliverance from wrath. Believers have no part in the day of judgment.

> Because thou hast kept the word of my patience, I also will keep thee from the hour of temptation, which shall come upon all the world, to try them that dwell upon the earth (Rev. 3:10).

"Out of" may be understood to mean complete exemption from the tribulation according to the context and other references requiring this meaning. "Hour" means not merely from temptation as such, but from the hour itself, the period of time in which the temptation takes place.

> Watch ye therefore, and pray always, that ye may be accounted worthy to escape all these things that shall come to pass, and to stand before the Son of man (Luke 21:36; cf. 21:25-35).
>
> Much more then, being now justified by his blood, we shall be saved from wrath through him (Rom. 5:9).

4. There will be some who are "alive and remain" at the coming of the Lord, according to 1 Thessalonians 4:15. Since all those who do not worship Antichrist during the tribulation are slain (Rev. 13:7, 8, 14, 15; 16:2; 19:20, 21; 20:4), no believers would be "alive and remain" if the Church should go through the great tribulation.

5. The Scriptures urge an attitude of constant expectation of Christ's second coming. If the Church goes through the tribulation, then believers would be looking for tribulation signs and events rather than Christ's return.

> And not only they, but ourselves also, which have the first-fruits of the Spirit, even we ourselves groan within ourselves, waiting for the adoption, to wit, the redemption of our body (Rom. 8:23).
>
> So that ye come behind in no gift: waiting for the coming of our Lord Jesus Christ (1 Cor. 1:7).
>
> For we through the Spirit wait for the hope of righteousness by faith (Gal. 5:5).

6. God has always protected His people before judgment fell. By analogy, illustration, and type, the Church too will be delivered before the final judgment.

    a. Enoch was translated before the judgment of the flood.

    b. Lot was taken out of Sodom before the judgment of Sodom and Gomorrah. Lot is a type of the Church (2 Peter 2:6-8).

    c. Noah was in the ark before the judgment of the flood. Noah is a type of the nation Israel, as being not kept from it, but saved while going through it (Jer. 30:7).

    d. The firstborn among the Hebrews in Egypt were sheltered by the blood of the Paschal lamb before judgment.

    e. Spies were safely out of Jericho and Rahab was secured before the judgment of Jericho.

    f. The Man-Child (Christ) in Revelation 12, who is caught up, is a symbol of the mystical Christ, the Church, being raptured.

7. Those of Paul's epistles written primarily for the instruction of the Church contain no warning to the Church that she must go through the great tribulation.

8. If the Church goes through the tribulation, then the Jews as well as the Gentiles of the tribulation period would become part of the Church. After the tribulation the

Jewish remnant would go on into their promised earthly millennial glory, whereas the Gentile element of the Church, having no expectation of earthly glory, would be caught up to be with Christ. This would dismember the body of Christ, which is inconceivable (Eph. 5:27).

9. Why would the Thessalonians be concerned that those who died would be at disadvantage, if those who were alive had to go through a time of wrath? Better would it be that they had died also.

10. The seven churches of Revelation 2 and 3 represent in some respects the seven periods of Church history from Pentecost till the end of the age. The Laodicean church, being last, could never go through the tribulation and still be called "luke-warm." For tribulation, as history has shown, has generally resulted in an ice-cold or red-hot church.

11. The message of the Church is a Gospel of grace. During the Tribulation period two witnesses, not of the Church, but of the Jews (as indicated by the sackcloth they wear), take up a message of judgment. Two different messages, one of grace and another of judgment cannot exist side by side. Some say that the gospel of the kingdom (millennial) and of judgment is also preached by the 144,000 Jewish remnant (Rev. 11:3; 7:4-8; 12:17; 19:10; Matt. 24:14).

12. Iniquity or lawlessness cannot set in in fullest measure until that which restrains it is removed. The restrainer is the Holy Spirit who manifests Himself to the world in and through the Church. Hence, before the revelation of the Antichrist, who is the "lawless one," the Church must be removed.

13. The Church cannot possibly be on earth during the tribulation and be slain for its testimony since the Church is instructed to pray for God's blessing on those in authority (1 Tim. 2:2). Those who were slain during the tribulation pray for the destruction of those in authority (Rev. 6:10).

These, then, are Jews praying vengeance on their enemies, as David prayed in the imprecatory Psalms (Ps. 31:17, 18).

14. Christ's coming *for* His Church is unconditional. His coming to earth, however, is conditioned by the sign of the setting up of the abomination of desolation three and a half years before His coming. The Church will be raptured before any definite sign.

> I will come again, and receive you unto myself; that where I am, there ye may be also (John 14:3). (The text does not say, "where you are, down on earth," but "where I am, up in heaven," there "ye may be also.")

> When ye therefore shall see the abomination of desolation spoken of by Daniel the prophet, stand in the holy place, (whoso readeth, let him understand:) Then let them which be in Judea flee into the mountains (Matt. 24:15, 16).

15. The inspired division of Revelation indicates the removal of the Church. Revelation 1:9 divides the book into: (1) things which John had seen: chapter 1; (2) things which are at present: chapters 2 and 3; (3) things which shall be "after these things": chapters 4-22. The expression "after these things" (4:1) means after the things of the Church in chapters 2 and 3 are historically past. There is no mention of the Church after chapters 2 and 3.

16. The multitude in Revelation 7 cannot be the Church because of reason #15 above and also because Revelation 7:15 states concerning this multitude that "He that sitteth on the throne shall tabernacle (literally) over them" whereas the place of the Church is *on* the throne.

17. The Church is seen in Revelation 4 as already in heaven, represented by the twenty-four elders. Their rapture to heaven was prefigured by John's transportation there. That the Church is represented by the twenty-four elders is supported by the following facts:

  a. They wear crowns, which speak of victory in conflict. Coronation time is at the resurrection. The redeemed alone are promised crowns (1 Cor. 9:25; 1 Thess. 2:19; 2 Tim. 2:12).

b. They are clothed in white raiment: "fine linen is the righteousness of the saints" (Rev. 19:8). White garments are promised to the redeemed (Rev. 2:10; 3:11; Isa. 61:10).

c. They sing a redemption song (5:9, 10): "Thou hast redeemed *us*. . . ." This text is supported by the Textus Receptus, Codex Sinaiticus (fourth century), Codex Basilianus (eighth century), Minuscule 1 (of uncertain date), and several other minuscules of late date, the Coptic, Latin, and Armenian (fifth century) versions, and quoted by Cyprian, Bishop of Carthage (A.D. 248), and by Primasius (sixth century).

"And hast made *us*. . . ." (v. 9). This is supported by the Textus Receptus, Codex Fuldensis (sixth century Latin version), Codex Coislinianus (tenth century), and quoted by Arethas, Bishop of Caesarea in Cappadocia (tenth century).

"And *we* shall reign on the earth. . . ." (10). This text is supported by the Textus Receptus, Mss. Demidovianus (twelfth century), Mss. Lipsienses (fourteenth and fifteenth centuries), and quoted by Arethas (tenth century), Primasius (sixth century), Julius Firmicus (A.D. 345), Idacius (the name under which Vigilius of Thapsis, A.D. 484 published his work.)

d. Even if the elders did sing, "Thou hast redeemed *them*," as some manuscripts read, the elders could sing of themselves objectively in the third person as the Israelites sang of themselves in their redemption from Egypt (Exod. 15:13, 16, 17).

e. They were from "every tribe, and tongue, and people, and nation" (5:9).

f. They are already in heaven when heaven received the multitude out of the great tribulation (7:14).

g. They are distinguished from the angels and from the four living creatures (5:11; 7:11).

h. The word "elders" is used in a representative sense

in the New Testament with respect to the Church (Titus 1:5).

  i. The number twenty-four would indicate their representing both Old and New Testament believers: twelve for the number of the tribes of Israel and twelve for the number of the Apostles. This interpretation is suggested by the analogy with Revelation 21 where names of the twelve tribes are written on the gates of New Jerusalem; and the names of the twelve Apostles, on the twelve foundations.

  j. John, as a symbol of the raptured Church, was only an onlooker of the events transpiring during the tribulation. He did not participate in the events, which followed his being raptured to heaven.

18. Christ's relation to the Church is as the "bright and morning star" (Rev. 22:16). His relation to Israel is as the "Sun of righteousness" (Mal. 4:2). Christ's coming for His saints is like the morning star, which is seen by few, whereas His revelation to the Jews is like the sun, which is evident to all.

19. The last trump, mentioned by Paul (1 Cor. 15:52), refers to the rapture of the believers. The last of the seven trumps in Revelation introduces the last half of Daniel's week. The two are not identical because:

  a. Paul speaks to the Church, not to Israel, in the Corinthian epistle.

  b. The seventh trump in Revelation is last only in its relation to the series.

  c. Paul speaks of "last" in Corinthians as the trump which brings to a close the Church age.

  d. Paul's trump is "the trump of God"; the trump in Revelation is sounded by an angel.

20. The entire Church, and not only a more faithful and vigilant part, will be raptured before the tribulation because:

    a. The Church is Christ's Body which cannot be dismembered.

    b. The Church is Christ's Bride. Will any part of His Bride be left?

    c. There will be some who are ashamed of His coming. This indicates that even faithless and carnal believers will be raptured, along with faithful ones (1 Cor. 3:15; 9:27; 1 John 2:28).

    d. If only the faithful, vigilant believers are taken, then those asleep in Christ who were faithful and vigilant have no advantage, for all the dead in Christ without discrimination are caught up (1 Thess. 4:14).

21. The Lord does not come to earth, but meets the saints *in the air* (1 Thess. 4:16). His coming for Israel at the end of the tribulation will be *to the earth* to set up His kingdom.

> And His feet shall stand in that day upon the mount of Olives. . . . And the Lord shall be king over all the earth (Zech. 14:4, 9).

22. The coming of the Lord is at a time of "peace and safety" (1 Thess. 5:3). In Revelation 5 at the opening of the first seal, the day of the Lord, the day of wrath, begins, and the day of grace ends. Therefore, the Church was raptured in Revelation 4 at the beginning of the day of the Lord when there was "peace and safety."

23. The rapture will be secret. The manifestation or public showing of His parousia (presence) takes place *after* the tribulation when Antichrist is destroyed.

> And then shall that Wicked be revealed, whom the Lord shall consume with the spirit of his mouth, and shall destroy with the brightness of his coming (2 Thess 2:8).

24. The rapture symbolized in the parable of the wheat and tares (Matt. 13) does not apply to the Church, but to Israel. The parable concerns the tribulation period. The good seed of the parable are the 144,000 Israelites, the children

of the kingdom, who are sown by God at that time. The harvest will be the ingathering of Israel.

   a. The Church is never called children of the kingdom. The parable of the Sower represents the Church age with God sowing His Word; the parable of the wheat and tares represents the tribulation period with God sowing the 144,000 Israelites.

   b. Angels do not gather the Church at the rapture; Christ comes alone.

25. The character of God as a God of grace demands that the Church escape the tribulation. The great majority of the Church have already escaped by dying and going to heaven. Why then should a small group left at the end times be subjected to this awful tribulation?

26. The Church age must be ended and the Church raptured before God begins to deal with the Jews. In Daniel's seventieth week, which records the history of God's dealing with Israel, there is no mention of the Church.

C. *An interval of time between His coming* FOR *and His coming* WITH *His saints is required for the judgment of the believers and the marriage supper of the Lamb to take place.*

These two events will take time, which is allowed by the Church's rapture before the tribulation.

### Bibliography

Armerding, Carl. *The Four and Twenty Elders.* New York: Loizeaux Brothers, no date.

Anderson, A. A. *Kommentarier over Uppenbarelssbaken.* Minneapolis: Standard Press, 1929.

Barnhouse, Donald Grey. *Revelation.* Grand Rapids, Michigan: Zondervan Publishing House, 1971.

Criswell, W. A. *Expository Sermons on Revelation.* Grand Rapids, Michigan: Zondervan Publishing House, 1962.

Darby, J. N. *Will the Saints Be in the Tribulation?* New York: Loizeaux Brothers, no date.

English, E. Schuyler. *Re-thinking the Rapture.* Travelers Rest, South Carolina: Southern Bible Book House, 1954.

Gortner, J. Narver. *Are the Saints Scheduled to Go Through the Tribulation?* Springfield, Missouri: Gospel Publishing House, no date.

Hamilton, Gavin. *Will the Church Escape the Great Tribulation?* New York: Loizeaux Brothers, 1944.

Hogg, C. F., and W. E. Vine. *The Church and the Tribulation.* London: Pickering and Inglis, no date.

Hottel, W. S. *The Lord Coming For and With His Saints.* Grand Rapids, Michigan: Zondervan Publishing House, 1937.

Ironside, H. A. *The Lamp of Prophecy.* Grand Rapids, Michigan: Zondervan Publishing House, 1940.

————. *Not Wrath, But Rapture.* New York: Loizeaux Brothers, no date.

Laidlaw, Robert A. *Will the Church Go Through the Great Tribulation?* New York: Loizeaux Brothers, no date.

Lantz, P. G. *Da Forsamlingen ar upptagen.* Chicago: 926 Buena Avenue, no date.

Lindsey, Hal. *The Late Great Planet Earth.* Grand Rapids, Michigan: Zondervan Publishing House, 1970.

MacArthur, Harry, E. McClelland Stuart, Britton Ross, and Keith L. Brooks. *Papers of the Rapture.* Los Angeles: American Prophetic League, 1940.

Marsh, F. E. *Will the Church, or Any Part of It, Go Through the Great Tribulation?* London: Pickering and Inglis, 1894.

Newell, William R. "Will the Church Go Through the Tribulation," *The Book of Revelation.* Chicago: Grace Publications, 1935.

Pache, Reve. *The Return of Jesus Christ,* trans. William S. Sa Sor. Chicago: Moody Press, 1955.

Panton, D. M. "Are We in the Great Tribulation?" *The Dawn,* 12:485-90 (February 15, 1936).

Pentecost, J. Dwight. *Prophecy for Today.* Grand Rapids, Michigan: Zondervan Publishing House, 1965.

Stanton, Gerard B. *Kept From the Hour.* Grand Rapids, Michigan: Zondervan Publishing House, 1956.

Strauss, Lehman. *God's Plan for the Future.* Grand Rapids, Michigan: Zondervan Publishing House, 1965.

Strombeck, J. F. *First the Rapture.* Moline, Illinois: Strombeck Agency, 1950.

Thiessen, Henry C. *Will the Church Pass Through the Tribulation?* New York: Loizeaux Brothers, 1941.

Walvoord, John F. *Fifty Arguments for Pretribulation,* Minneapolis: Central Conservative Baptist Seminary, no date.

————. *The Rapture Question.* Grand Rapids, Michigan: Dunham Publishing Company, 1957.

Whiting, Arthur B. "The Rapture of the Church," *Bibliotheca Sacra,* 102: 360-72 July, 1945); 102:49-99 (October, 1945).

Wood, Leon J. *Is the Rapture Next?* Grand Rapids, Michigan: Zondervan Publishing House, 1956.

# MID-TRIBULATION RAPTURE

Those who affirm this view of the time of the rapture hold essentially the same position as the pre-tribulationist with the exception that the interval of time between the Lord's coming *for* His saints and His coming *with* them is shortened. Instead of placing the rapture in Revelation 4, mid-tribulationists place the rapture between the second and third woes in Revelation. Their reasons are as follows:

1. The last trumpet of Paul and the seventh trumpet of Revelation are identical. They sound in the middle of the tribulation period (the seventieth week of Daniel) since both announce a resurrection. Therefore, the rapture must be at that time (1 Cor. 15:52; Rev. 11:15; 1 Thess. 4:16, 17).

2. The great tribulation is only the last half of Daniel's seventieth week (Rev. 11:2, 3; 12:6, 14).

3. "A little book" in the hand of the coming Lord in Revelation 10:1, 2 is the introduction of these events which close the Jewish age. The seven seals and trumpets fulfilled the Church age before the rapture. At this point John is no longer an onlooker, but participates in the coming scenes; he is required to eat the little book; his eating symbolizes what Israel is to experience.

4. The seals are not direct judgments, but according to Matthew 24:3-12, indicate simply the "*beginning* of sorrows" which precede the great tribulation.

5. To pre-tribulationists John's rapture to heaven is symbolic of the Church's rapture (Rev. 4). To mid-tribulationists the resurrection of the two witnesses is symbolic of the rapture of the Church (Rev. 11:3-13).

   a. The two witnesses are called two olive trees (Rev. 11:4).

   b. The olive trees represent Old and New Testament saints (Rom. 11:13-25).

   c. All witnessing, the distinctive mission of the Church, ceases with the rapture of the two witnesses.

6. The Day of Wrath is mentinoned as at hand in Revelation 11:18; therefore, the preceding seals and trumpets were not events of wrath.

Some hold that the time of the rapture is revealed in Revelation 14:14-16 because: (1) of the similarity of this passage with 1 Thessalonians 4:16, 17 which definitely refers to the rapture; and (2) the Church, according to the promise of Revelation 3:10, will escape, not the "day" but the "hour" of judgment which arrives in Revelation 14:7 prior to the outpouring of the wrath of God in the seven bowls of Revelation 15 and 16.

### Bibliography

Harrison, Norman R. *The End: Re-Thinking the Revelation.* Minneapolis: The Harrison Service, 1941.

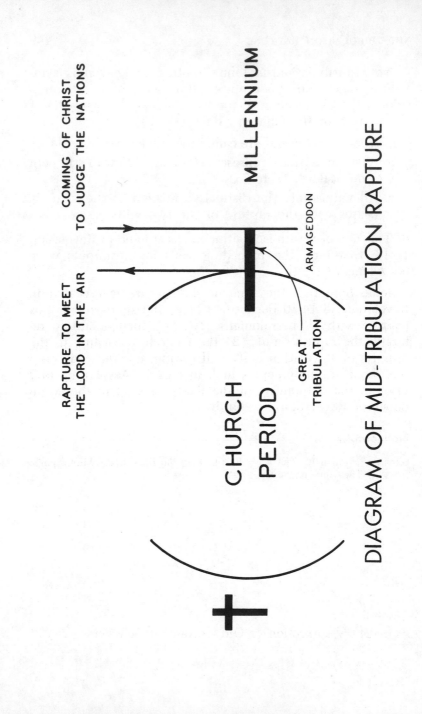

RAPTURE TO MEET THE LORD IN THE AIR

COMING OF CHRIST TO JUDGE THE NATIONS

MILLENNIUM

CHURCH PERIOD

GREAT TRIBULATION

ARMAGEDDON

DIAGRAM OF MID-TRIBULATION RAPTURE

# POST-TRIBULATION RAPTURE

Those who affirm this view of the time of the rapture believe that the second coming of Christ and the rapture are parts of the same event. The second coming of Christ will be a day of judgment for the beast, the false prophet, and the armies of the nations. For the Church and repentant Israel it will be a day of glory. The Scriptures which refer to this coming of Christ include various expressions: *parousia, or presence, the day of Christ, the day of the Lord Jesus Christ, the day of the Lord, the coming, the revelation, the epiphany or appearing,* and *the coming of the Son of man.*

The Church will not be raptured until this manifestation of Christ at the end of the tribulation period. While believers will not be subject to the outpouring of the *wrath of God,* being sealed in protection, they may be exposed to the *persecution of Antichrist* during the tribulation.

Those who hold to a post-tribulation rapture affirm the following:

1. The rapture of the Church, the living saints, and the resurrection and rapture of those dead in Christ of both Old and New Testament believers, will take place at the public revelation of Christ at the end of the tribulation period.

   a. The resurrection of Old Testament believers (Isa. 26:19) takes place at the day of the Lord (Isa. 24:21; 26:1), after the great tribulation (Isa. 24:16 - 25:9).

At the conversion of Israel (Isa. 25:9; 26:12-15), at the establishment of the Messianic kingdom (Isa. 25: 6-8; 26:1-9), and at the time of signs in the heavens (Isa. 24:23).

b. The resurrection of Old Testament believers takes place after the great tribulation (Dan. 12:1); at the time when Antichrist is destroyed (Dan. 11:45); at the time when Israel shall be delivered from her trouble (Dan. 12:1).

c. Daniel's personal resurrection will take place at the "end," which evidently refers to the "end" mentioned so often in the book of Daniel: end of Antichrist and his career (Dan. 7:26; 9:26); end of the times of the Gentiles (Dan. 8:17, 19).

d. The resurrection of believers takes place "at the last day" of this present age, before the kingdom age (millennium) (John 6:39, 40, 44, 54; 11:24). The New Testament recognizes only two ages: (1) the present age, pre-Kingdom or pre-Messianic (Mark 10:30; Rom. 8:18; 1 Tim. 6:19; Gal. 1:4); and (2) the age to come, the future Kingdom age, or Messianic age (Luke 20: 35; Mark 10:30; Matt. 13:32; Heb. 6:5).

e. The millennial age and the resurrection are linked together (Luke 20:34-36).

f. The transfiguration of the believers occurs at a time when sinners and stumbling blocks are rooted out of the kingdom (Matt. 13:41-43).

g. The resurrection is mentioned in connection with eating bread in the millennial kingdom (Luke 14:14, 15).

h. The resurrection at the last trump and the transfiguration that takes place then is the fulfillment of Isaiah 25:8: "Death is swallowed up in victory." The context of this Old Testament passage states that the resurrection occurs at the day of the Lord, at the conversion of Israel, after the great tribulation, and at the establishment of the Messianic kingdom (1 Cor. 15:50-54).

i. The resurrection is linked with the conversion of Israel, which is generally held to be at the end of the tribulation (Rom. 11:15).

j. The dead in Christ will be at no disadvantage but rather will be raised first, and then the living believers will be caught up with them to meet the Lord. Both Old and New Testament believers will be raptured, thus, at the same time (1 Thess. 4:13-18).

k. The order of the resurrection will be:
Christ — the firstfruits
The redeemed — at Christ's return
Then the END (which, because of the preceding context, refers to the last or third phase of the resurrection, namely, the wicked dead (Rev. 20:5). Thus, there is no room for two resurrections of believers: a resurrection of the redeemed at the beginning and another resurrection of the redeemed at the end of the tribulation period (1 Cor. 15:21-26).

l. The first resurrection takes place at Christ's return when He destroys Antichrist and the armies of the world, when Satan is bound, and when Christ inaugurates the millennial kingdom (Rev. 20:4-6). At this time three groups of believers are resurrected:

(1) those who sat upon thrones
(2) the souls of those beheaded for their testimony
(3) those that did not worship the beast

If a prior resurrection of seven years or more before the millennium existed, why did John call this one the first one?

2. The parable of the wheat and tares of Matthew 13 shows the position of the Church in the world at the end time.

a. "Wheat" refers to Christians, the sons of God; "tares" refers to unbelievers, the sons of the evil one.

b. Both grow together until the harvest, which is the consummation of the age (verse 39).

c. Bible teachers who hold the post-tribulation rapture view believe that the consummation of the age is at the time of Christ's second coming (Matt. 24:3). They cite the omission of the article preceding "end" in Matthew 24:3 in support of their view. The omission of the article would indicate the identity of His coming and the consummation of the age. "End of the age," they affirm, cannot mean an indefinitely lengthened period since "the harvest" is the end of the age. The angel reapers cast the things which offend into a furnace of fire; there will be wailing and gnashing of teeth. It would be very unlikely that Antichrist would arise after this. Also, at the end of the age "the righteous shine forth as the sun in the kingdom of their Father."

3. The great commission (Matt. 28:19, 20) indicates that the Church will be in the world at the consummation of the age. This commission is for the Church and not a Jewish remnant, as represented by the disciples because: (a) the commission was given after Christ's resurrection, and (b) Christ revealed Himself after the resurrection only to believers who were redeemed by His blood and in union with Him. To these He promised His glorified, risen presence even until *the end of the age*.

4. The word "end," meaning final end of the age, appears in the New Testament epistles in connection with the Church. This is further evidence that the Church is in the world at the end of the age. The "end" is in connection with the revelation and day of Christ toward which the Corinthian Church would be confirmed (1 Cor. 1:7, 8; cf. Heb. 3:6, 14; 6:11). Also believers who are victorious over trials and who keep Christ's works to the "end" will be rewarded (Rev. 2:26). This promise is given in context of His coming in the clouds, immediately preceding the millennial kingdom (Rev. 2:25; 1:7; 2:27).

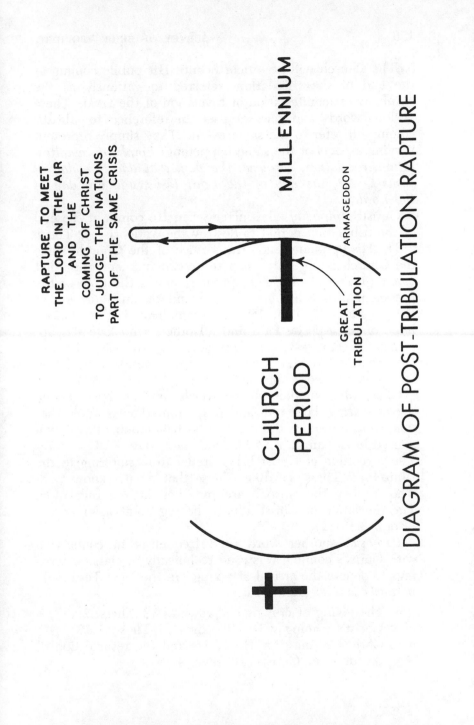

RAPTURE TO MEET
THE LORD IN THE AIR
AND THE
COMING OF CHRIST
TO JUDGE THE NATIONS
PART OF THE SAME CRISIS

MILLENNIUM

ARMAGEDDON

GREAT
TRIBULATION

CHURCH
PERIOD

DIAGRAM OF POST-TRIBULATION RAPTURE

5. The Church will be on earth until His public coming at the end of the tribulation, referred to variously as the epiphany or manifestation or revelation of the Lord. These various words and phrases used in reference to Christ's coming all refer to the same event. They simply represent varying aspects of the same happening: *epiphany, manifestation, revelation, parousia, the day, that day, the day of Jesus Christ, the day of the Lord Jesus, and the day of the Lord.*

Christ's *epiphany* takes place when He comes at the end of the tribulation period to destroy the Antichrist (2 Thess. 2:8). His epiphany ends the service of the Church, since the Church is urged to keep the commandment until that event (1 Tim. 6:14). His epiphany marks the time of the judgment of the living and dead and the inauguration of His kingdom (2 Tim. 4:1). His epiphany is the glorious hope of the Apostle Paul and all others who love His appearing (2 Tim. 4:8). His epiphany and "the blessed hope" are identified by the vinculum of a common article, i.e. "the (blessed hope and appearance)" (Titus 2:13).

Concerning another of the words used of His coming, the *revelation,* both pre- and post-tribulationists agree that this event occurs at the end of the tribulation. Revelation is used interchangeably with "end" and "day" (1 Cor. 1:7). The revelation of Christ brings relief from suffering to the Church (2 Thess. 1:5-10). Those that do not know God, who disobey the Gospel, are punished at His revelation. The revelation of Christ affects the regeneration of nature (Rom. 8:18-23).

*Parousia,* another word used frequently in connection with Christ's coming, was used technically in classical writings to denote the arrival of a king. In the New Testament *parousia* is associated with:

a. The giving of crowns and rewards (1 Thess. 2:19);
b. Christ's coming with His saints (1 Thess. 3:13);
c. Christ's coming for His saints and the resurrection of the dead in Christ (1 Thess. 4:19);

d. The holiness of the Church in preparation for the day (1 Thess. 5:23);
e. The gathering of the elect (2 Thess. 2:1);
f. The overthrow of Antichrist and the manifestation of Christ (2 Thess. 2:8);
g. The resurrection and transfiguration of the redeemed when the kingdom is established (1 Cor. 15:23, 50-52);
h. The coming and kingdom of the Son of man (2 Peter 1:16; cf. Matt. 16:28 - 17:8);
i. The day of God (2 Peter 3:12);
j. The public manifestation of Christ (1 John 2:28);

Other words that refer to His second coming are used less frequently than *epiphany, revelation,* and *parousia.* At *the day* unbelievers will be taken by surprise, but believers will be expecting Christ (1 Thess. 5:4). At *the day* also the works of saints will be judged, an event recorded as happening at:

a. His manifestation and kingdom (2 Tim. 4:1-8);
b. The parousia (1 Thess. 2:19 - 3:13);
c. The last trump (Rev. 11:18);
d. The last day (John 6:39-54);
e. His coming as Son of man (Matt. 16:27).

Appearances in the New Testament of the other words referring to His second coming are as follows: *that day* (2 Thess. 1:10; 2 Tim. 1:12, 18; 4:8); *the day of Jesus Christ* (Phil. 1:6, 10; 2:16); the *day of the Lord Jesus* (1 Cor. 1:7, 8; 2 Cor. 1:14); the *day of the Lord* (1 Thess. 5:2; 2 Thess. 2:1-3). Concerning this last reference, there are two signs given by Paul which must take place before the *day of the Lord:* the "falling away" and the revelation of the Man of Sin. The Thessalonians worried that they had missed the day of the Lord. Paul corrected their misconception by reminding them of the two events which precede Christ's coming. From this passage it is evident that the Thessalonians still awaited the *day of the Lord,* even after they read 1 Thessalonians 4:14, which is supposed to teach a secret rapture preceding the day. Why did not Paul soothe their laments by referring to that rapture as a necessary precursor of the day of the Lord instead of referring to the Apostasy and the Man of Sin as precursors?

6. The promise of deliverance — "keep thee from the hour of temptation" (Rev. 3:10) — does not necessitate a rapture of the Church to heaven for fulfillment (Alexander Reese, Norman McPherson).

   a. The word "out of," translated from the Greek preposition *ek*, is not conclusive, as admitted by all Greek scholars. "*Ek*" means "out of the midst" of the interior of a thing. The Greek preposition "*apo*" would have been better used to express immunity, for *apo* means "away from" the side of a thing.

   b. "Them that dwell on the earth." The intensive form of "dwell" in the original cannot be conclusive evidence that these people deliberately chose the earth as a permanent abode rather than heaven. The same word is used of our Lord "dwelling" in Capernaum (Matt. 4:13).

   c. Deliverance from the wrath of God can be accomplished even in the sphere of that wrath. The locusts of the tribulation period are forbidden to touch the sealed ones (Rev. 9:4). Deliverance from divine wrath does not necessarily confer deliverance from Satanic wrath.

   d. If the Church is not here at the time of the tribulation period, then why the promises in verses 11 and 12?

7. Christ's coming is not imminent, but contingent on the fulfillment of certain events:

   a. The great commission; the Gospel preached in all the world for a witness (Matt. 28:19, 20; 24:14);

   b. The parables of Matthew 13;

   c. Jesus' prediction of Peter's martyrdom (John 21:19-23);

d. Paul's provision for permanent organization of the Church and its continued ministry;

e. The rise of apostasy (2 Thess. 2:8);

f. The revelation of the Man of Sin (2 Thess. 2:8).

8. Heaven received Christ *until the restitution of all things* (Acts 3:21), which will take place after the tribulation, according to both pre-tribulationists and post-tribulationists.

9. The Marriage Supper takes place at the end of the tribulation after Babylon is destroyed if Revelation is in chronological order.

10. The twenty-four elders are heavenly kings who lead the worship in heaven, not a group representative of the Church in heaven.

a. John saw the elders sitting there in heaven when he ascended to heaven. They had not just sat down when John first saw the vision.

b. They do not sing a redemption song, but sing about others, from every tribe, tongue, and nation, who have been redeemed, according to the best manuscripts: "Thou hast redeemed *us.* . . ." The word "us" is omitted by Codex Alexandrinus of the fifth century. ". . . and made *them* to be a kingdom and priests to God, and *they* shall reign upon the earth." This is supported by Codex Sinaiticus (fourth or fifth century), Codex St. Petersburg (ninth century), Codices Lipsienses (fourteenth or fifteenth century), Mss. Amianthius (A.D. 551-700), Mss. Fuldensis (sixth century), Mss. Harleianus, No. 1772 (ninth century), Mss. Toletanus (eighth century), Coptic and Latin versions, and quoted by Andreas and Arethas.

c. Those who interpret these elders other than as literal must have scriptural proof for their symbolism rather than mere conjecture.

d. If the elders are symbolic, by the same reasoning, then also are the four living creatures symbolic, and so one, *ad infinitum.*

## Bibliography

Fraser, Alexander. *The Return of Christ in Glory.* Pittsburgh: The Evangelical Fellowship, 1950.

Fromow, George H. *Will the Church Pass Through the Tribulation?* London: Sovereign Grace Advent Testimony, no date.

Frost, Henry W. *Matthew Twenty-four and the Revelation.* New York: Oxford University Press, 1924.

—————. *The Second Coming of Christ.* Grand Rapids, Michigan: William B. Eerdmans, 1934.

Gordon, A. J. *Ecce Venit.* New York: Fleming Revell, 1889.

Graham, James R. *Watchman, What of the Night?* Los Angeles: Ambassadors for Christ, no date.

Ladd, George E. *The Blessed Hope.* Grand Rapids, Michigan: William B. Eerdmans, 1956.

McPherson, Norman S. *Triumph Through Tribulation.* Otego, New York, 1944.

Morris, Leon. *The Epistles of Paul to the Thessalonians.* Grand Rapids, Michigan: William B. Eerdmans, 1957.

Ockenga, Harold J. "Will the Church Go Through the Tribulation? Yes," *Christian Life.* 16:10 (February, 1955).

—————. "Fulfilled and Unfulfilled Prophecy," *Prophecy in the Making,* ed. Carl F. H. Henry. Wheaton, Illinois: Creation House, 1971.

Payne, J. Barton. *The Imminent Appearing of Christ.* Grand Rapids, Michigan: William B. Eerdmans, 1962.

Reese, Alexander. *The Approaching Advent of Christ.* London: Marshall, Morgan, and Scott, no date.

Rose, George L. *Tribulation Till Translation.* Glendale, California: Rose Publishing Company, 1943.

# RESTORATION OF ISRAEL

## Old Testament Promises of Israel's Return to Palestine

And it shall come to pass in that day, that the Lord shall set his hand again the second time to recover the remnant of his people, which shall be left, from Assyria, and from Egypt, and from Pathros, and from Cush, and from Elam, and from Shinar, and from Hamath, and from the islands of the sea (Isa. 11:11).

And there is hope in thine end, saith the Lord, that thy children shall come again to their own border. . . . Yea, I will rejoice over them to do them good, and I will plant them in this land assuredly with my whole heart and with my whole soul. For thus saith the Lord: Like as I have brought all this great evil upon this people, so will I bring upon them the good that I have promised them (Jer. 31: 17; 32:41, 42).

Therefore, behold, the days come, saith the Lord, that it shall no more be said, The Lord liveth, that brought up the children of Israel out of the land of Egypt; but, The Lord liveth, that brought up the children of Israel from the land of the north, and from all the lands whither he had driven them: and I will bring them again into their land that I gave unto their fathers (Jer. 16:14, 15).

And say unto them, Thus saith the Lord God; Behold, I will take the children of Israel from among the heathen, whither they be gone, and will gather them on every side, and bring them unto their own land (Ezek. 37:21). (Compare also Jer. 23:3; 24:6-9; Ezek. 37:25; Amos 9:14, 15; Zech. 10:10.)

161

### Basis of Return

1. *Conditional on Israel's doing God's will*

   a. On obedience to the Lord (Deut. 30:2-5).
   b. On keeping the Sabbath (Jer. 17:24-27).
   c. On repentance and obedience (Jer. 18:7-10).
   d. On doing righteousness, relieving oppression, and doing no wrong to strangers, to the fatherless, or to widows, nor shedding innocent blood (Jer. 22:1-5).

Israel's return would have taken place sooner had they fulfilled the conditions of doing God's will. But in spite of Israel's failure, they will receive the blessings promised by God unconditionally for the sake of His name.

2. *The unconditional grace of God*

> But I had pity for mine holy name, which the house of Israel had profaned among the heathen, whither they went. Therefore say unto the house of Israel, Thus saith the Lord God; I do not this for your sakes, O house of Israel, but for mine holy name's sake, which ye have profaned among the heathen whither ye went. And I will sanctify my great name, which was profaned among the heathen, which ye have profaned in the midst of them; and the heathen shall know that I am the Lord, saith the Lord God, when I shall be sanctified in you before their eyes. For I will take you from among the heathen, and gather you out of all countries, and will bring you into your own land. . . . Not for your sakes do I this, saith the Lord God, be it known unto you: be ashamed and confounded for your own ways, O house of Israel (Ezek. 36:21-24, 32). (Also Isa. 43:25; Ezek. 20:9, 14, 17, 22, 33-44.)

### Relation of Israel's Return to the Gentiles

The Gentiles will be amazed at God's work in Israel (see also 2a, b below). God will use the Gentiles to help restore Israel. He will punish the nations that mistreat Israel.

> Behold, I will lift up mine hand to the Gentiles, and set up my standard to the people: and they shall bring thy sons

in their arms, and thy daughters shall be carried upon their shoulders. And kings shall be thy nursing fathers, and their queens thy nursing mothers: they shall bow down to thee with their face toward the earth, and lick up the dust of thy feet; and thou shalt know that I am the Lord; for they shall not be ashamed that wait for me (Isa. 49:22, 23).

And the sons of strangers shall build up thy walls, and their kings shall minister unto thee (Isa. 60:10).

The nations shall see and be confounded at all their might: they shall lay their hand upon their mouth, their ears shall be deaf (Micah 7:16).

Also Isaiah 14:1, 2; 60:11, 14, 16; Jeremiah 12:14-17; Micah 4:11, 12; 7:17.

## Nature of the Restoration of Palestine

### 1. *Geographical changes*

a. The tongue of the Egyptian sea will be destroyed; men will go over dryshod. There will be a highway from Assyria (Isa. 11:14-16; 27:12).

b. The wilderness and the desert will blossom. There will be pools in parched grounds; springs in the lands; and grass, reeds, and rushes in the habitations of "dragon" (Isa. 35:1, 2, 7).

c. Sharon shall be a fold of flocks; the valley of Anchor, a place for herds (Isa. 65:8-10).

d. All rivers of Judah will flow with waters. A fountain will come forth out of the house of the Lord and will water the valley of Shittim (Joel 3:18). Literally, this is the "valley of Acacias" which perhaps may be: (1) the valley of Shittim, the last encampment of Israel on the east side of the Jordan before their entrance into Canaan (Num. 25:1; Josh. 3:1); or (2) the valley of Acacias, a continuation of the Kidron down the Wady en Nar southeast of Jerusalem into the Dead Sea.

e. Edom and Egypt will be a desolate wilderness (Joel 3:18, 19).

f. Israel will possess the remnant of Edom (Amos 9:12).

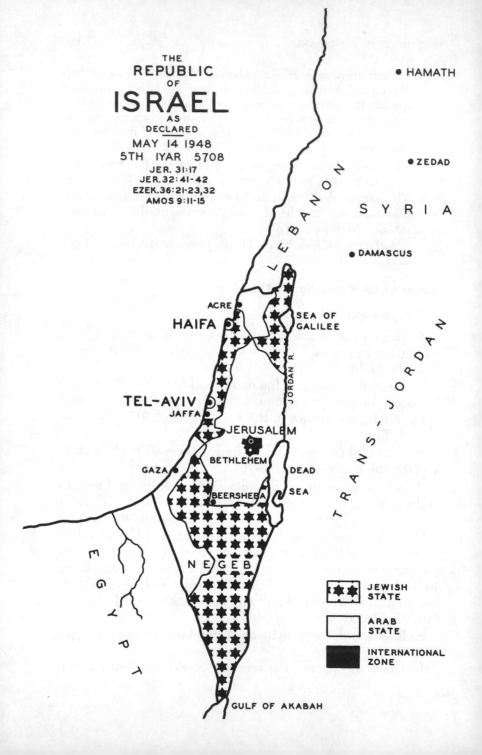

THE
REPUBLIC
OF
ISRAEL
AS
DECLARED
MAY 14 1948
5TH IYAR 5708
JER. 31:17
JER. 32:41-42
EZEK.36:21-23,32
AMOS 9:11-15

● HAMATH

● ZEDAD

S Y R I A

● DAMASCUS

LEBANON

ACRE
HAIFA
SEA OF
GALILEE

JORDAN R.

TEL-AVIV
JAFFA
JERUSALEM
BETHLEHEM
GAZA
BEERSHEBA
DEAD
SEA

T R A N S - J O R D A N

N E G E B

E G Y P T

✡ JEWISH
STATE

ARAB
STATE

■ INTERNATIONAL
ZONE

GULF OF AKABAH

g. Israel will possess the mount of Esau, the land of the Philistines, the fields of Ephraim, the fields of Samaria, Gilead (the tribe of Benjamin), into Zarephath and Sepharad (unknown, but perhaps in the region east of Assyria, north of Syria) (Obad. 18 - 20).

h. The coastal plain of Philistia, "the houses of Ashkelon," will be for Judah (Zeph. 2:7).

## 2. Political changes

a. Gentiles come into Israel's light: Midian, Ephah, Sheba, Kedar, Nebaioth, the isles, and Tarshish minister to Israel, as well as Philistia, Edom, Moab and Ammon (Isa. 11:14; 60:3-9, 16).

b. Nations who refuse to serve Israel will be wasted (Isa. 60:12; cf. 54:3).

c. The Lord is judge, lawgiver, and king of Israel. He will restore judges and counselors. The nobles will be chosen from among themselves. The governor will proceed from their midst. Righteousness and faithfulness will characterize Jerusalem (Isa. 1:26; Jer. 30:21; Obad. 21).

d. Judah and Israel will be united into one nation under one king, "David my servant." There will be everlasting peace (Isa. 11:13; Jer. 3:18; 23:5-8; 30:9; 33:17; Ezek. 34:23; 37:22, 24-28).

## 3. Social and economic changes

a. Bow, sword and battle will be taken out of the land (Hosea 2:18).

b. The land will be more fruitful and productive (Isa. 4:2; 29:17; 30:23-25; Ezek. 36:30; Hosea 2:21, 22; Joel 2:21-26; 3:18; Amos 9:13-15).

c. Fear, sorrow, and bondage will be removed; joy and merriment will abound (Micah 4:4; Isa. 35:10; 51:3, 11; 55:12; 61:3; Jer. 30:10; 31:13).

d. Israel will increase (Jer. 23:3; Isa. 60:22).

e. Great prosperity will characterize their restoration (Jer. 31:14).

f. There will be a vast building program (Ezek. 36:33-36).

## 4. Religious changes

a. Israel will turn to the Lord and be cleansed from sin (Isa. 33:24; 60:21; Jer. 30:22; Ezek. 36:33; Micah 4:5).

b. The sanctuary will be restored. The Levites will be cleansed from sin and will offer acceptable sacrifices (Ezek. 37:26; Amos 9:11; Isa. 66:21; Jer. 33:18; Mal. 3:3,4).

c. True, spiritual leaders will be set over them to feed them (Jer. 3:15; 23:4).

d. There will be a great outpouring of the Spirit (Joel 2:28, 29).

e. Jerusalem will be called the throne of the Lord, and all nations will be gathered to the name of the Lord (Jer. 3:17).

## Bibliography

Baron, David. *Israel's Inalienable Possession.* London: Marshall, Morgan and Scott, no date.

Chalmers, Thomas M. *Israel in Covenant and History.* New York: Author, 1926.

Ferrin, Howard W. "All Israel Shall Be Saved," *Bibliotheca Sacra,* 112: 235-47 (July, 1955).

Gaebelein, Arno C. *Hath God Cast Away His People?* New York: Gospel Publishing House, 1905.

Hendriksen, William. *And So All Israel Shall Be Saved.* Grand Rapids, Michigan: Baker Book House, 1945.

Kann, Herbert. "The History of Israel's Blindness: the Mystery of It," *Bibliotheca Sacra,* 94:442-57 (October, 1937).

Saphir, Adolph. *Christ and Israel.* London: Morgan, 1911.

Scofield, C. I. "The Return of Christ in Relation to the Jews and the Earth," *Bibliotheca Sacra,* 108:477-87 (October, 1951).

Thiessen, Henry C. "The Place of Israel in the Scheme of Redemption as Set Forth in Romans 9 - 11," *Bibliotheca Sacra,* 98:78-91 (January, 1941); 98:203-17 (April, 1941).

Walvoord, John F. "Israel's Restoration," *Bibliotheca Sacra,* 102:405-16 (October, 1945).

─────. "The New Covenant With Israel," *Bibliotheca Sacra,* 103:16-27 (January, 1946).

Washington, Canon M. *The Period of Judgment and the Saved Remnant.* London: Thynne, 1919.

Wilkinson, Samuel Hinds. *"Israel My Glory,"* London: Mildmay Mission to the Jews Book Store, 1894.

Witsius, Herman. *The Restitution of Israel.* London, 1840.

# RESURRECTION

## Definition

The word "resurrection" is used more than forty times in the New Testament in a uniform and exclusive sense to denote the "raising up" of the dead.

## Two Kinds of Resurrection

The Scriptures suggest a difference in kinds of resurrection. There will be two kinds of resurrection: (1) a resurrection of the just, known as a resurrection of life and a better resurrection; and (2) a resurrection of the wicked, known as the resurrection of damnation.

> Marvel not at this: for the hour is coming, in the which all that are in the graves shall hear his voice, and shall come forth; they that have done good, unto (the) resurrection of life; and they that have done evil, unto (the) resurrection of damnation (John 5:28, 29): (The articles in the Greek text are omitted.)

> But when thou makest a feast, call the poor, the maimed, the lame, the blind; and thou shalt be blessed; for they cannot recompense thee: for thou shalt be recompensed at the resurrection of the just (Luke 14:13, 14).

> Women received their dead raised to life again; and others were tortured, not accepting deliverance; that they might obtain a better resurrection (Heb. 11:35).

> That I may know him, and the power of his resurrection,

and the fellowship of his sufferings, being made conformable unto his death; if by any means I might attain unto the resurrection of the dead. (Literally, "the resurrection — the one out from the dead ones") (Phil. 3:10, 11). (If the Apostle Paul had in mind a resurrection of all the dead, how could he speak of attaining it "by any means," since he could not possibly escape it?" Scofield)

## The Order of Resurrections

The Scriptures suggest a definite order in the resurrections: (1) Christ the firstfruits; (2) they that are Christ's at His coming; and (3) the wicked dead (see POST-TRIBULATION RAPTURE, 1, i).

But every man in his own order: Christ the firstfruits; afterward they that are Christ's at his coming. Then cometh the end, when he shall have delivered up the kingdom to God, even the Father; when he shall have put down all rule and all authority and power. For he must reign, till he hath put all enemies under his feet (1 Cor. 15:23-25).

And I saw thrones, and they sat upon them, and judgment was given unto them: and I saw the souls of them that were beheaded for the witness of Jesus, and for the word of God, and which had not worshipped the beast, neither his image, neither had received his mark upon their foreheads, or in their hands; and they lived and reigned with Christ a thousand years. But the rest of the dead lived not again until the thousand years were finished. This is the first resurrection. Blessed and holy is he that hath part in the first resurrection: on such the second death hath no power, but they shall be priests of God and of Christ, and shall reign with him a thousand years (Rev. 20:4-6).

1. The first resurrection consists of those who reign with Christ a thousand years. They are:

a. Those who sat on thrones to whom judgment was given.

b. Those beheaded for the witness of Jesus and for the word of God.

c. Those who had not worshiped the beast, nor his image, nor received his mark on their foreheads nor on their hands.

2. The rest of the dead were not resurrected until the end of the thousand years when they appear before the great white throne.

## Old Testament Witness to the Resurrection

1. Abraham believed in the resurrection of the body (Heb. 11:19).
2. The son of the widow of Zarephath was raised from the dead by Elijah (1 Kings 17).
3. The Shunamite's son was raised from the dead (2 Kings 4:32-35).
4. A man who was being buried by the Moabites rose from the dead when his body touched Elisha's bones (2 Kings 13:20, 21).
5. Job believed in a resurrection of the body (Job 19:25-27).
6. David believed in a resurrection of the body (Ps. 16:10; 17:1).
7. Isaiah and Daniel prophesied concerning the future resurrection (Isa. 26:19; Dan. 12:1-3).

# SECOND COMING OF CHRIST

## Definition

The second coming of Christ refers to His personal and visible return to earth in glory. His return will be one of the greatest events in future time. This is one of the great doctrines of the Christian faith. So clear and distinct is the language used by the Lord in speaking of His return that it cannot be understood in any other way than in a literal and historic sense. The second coming of Christ will be one of the great vindications of the truth of Scripture before an unbelieving world that considers the Gospel message a failure.

The second coming of Christ is announced by Christ Himself (John 14:3; Matt. 24:29, 30), by angels (Acts 1: 11), and by the Apostles Peter and Paul in their epistles to the churches (Phil. 3:20; 1 Thess. 4:15, 16; Titus 2:13; 1 Peter 1:7, 13; Heb. 9:28).

## The Nature of the Second Coming

In the Authorized Version of the Bible there are several words used to describe the Lord's return, such as: His *coming*, His *appearing*, His *manifestation*, and His *revelation*. These are translations of the following Greek words:

1. *Come, ἔρχομαι.*
2. *Revelation, ἀποκάλυψις.*
3. *Manifestation, ἐπιφάνεια.*
4. *Presence, παρουσία.*

170

The first of these words, ἔρχομαι, meaning "to come" or "to go," is used in this ordinary manner about seven hundred times in the New Testament. Our Lord uses this word in reference also to His second coming (John 14:3): "I will come again, and receive you unto myself." The Apostle Paul also uses the word in reference to the Lord's second coming in speaking of the Lord's Supper that "ye do show the Lord's death till He come" (1 Cor. 11:26). Luke, too, records that the angels used the word in prophesying the Lord's return to earth (Acts 1:11): ". . . this same Jesus . . . shall so come in like manner as ye have seen him go into heaven."

In tracing this word ἔρχομαι through the New Testament, the following facts are stated about the second coming of Christ:

1. His coming will be as sudden and unexpected as Noah's flood. He will come as a "thief" and "in such an hour as ye think not" (Matt. 24:39, 42-44, 48, 50; 25:13; Luke 12:37-40).

2. After the great tribulation Christ will come (Matt. 24:29, 30).

3. Great disturbances in the sun, moon, and stars will accompany the event (Matt. 24:29; Mark 13:25, 26; Luke 21:25-27).

4. His coming will be in the clouds of heaven with power and great glory, at the sound of a trumpet and with angels (Matt. 24:20, 21; 26:64; Mark 13:26; 14:62; Luke 21:27).

5. Then every man will be rewarded according to his works. The hidden things of darkness will be brought out into the open. Christ will then be ashamed of those who have been ashamed of Him (Matt. 16:27; 1 Cor. 4:5; Mark 8:38; Luke 9:26).

6. All nations will be gathered before Him in judgment (Matt. 25:31, 32).

7. He will come with ten thousands of His saints (Jude 14).

8. Christ will bring in the kingdom, at which time also He will gather together His elect from one end of heaven to the other and from the four winds (Luke 21:27-31; Matt. 24:31).

The second word, ἀποκάλυψις, meaning "revelation," is a composite of two Greek words: ἀπό "away from" and καλύπτω "to cover" or "to hide." The word literally means "to draw away" the veil from; hence, "to lay bare" or "to reveal" something. The word is used of persons or events obscured from view and made visible as in a display of someone or something. For example, the word is used of a light that was in the person of Christ to appear to the Gentiles (Luke 21:32). In reference to the coming of the Lord, the word means literally that whatever has obscured or hidden Him from view will be drawn away. In the Authorized Version the word is translated variously as *manifestation* (Rom. 8:19), *coming* (1 Cor. 1:7); *revelation* (1 Peter 1:13); *appearing* (1 Peter 1:7); *to lighten* (Luke 2:32).

In tracing the word ἀποκάλυψις through the New Testament, we discover the following facts about the second coming of Christ:

1. The revelation is identified with the end of the age (1 Cor. 1:7, 8) and with the day of wrath and the righteous judgment of God (Rom 2:5).

2. The revelation of Christ will bring to the saints relief from suffering and tribulation (2 Thess. 1:7).

3. Christ will be accompanied with mighty angels. He will come in flaming fire and in vengeance to be glorified in His saints (2 Thess. 1:7, 8, 10).

4. The second coming of Christ will become an incentive for holy living, a motive to the believer for the diligent use of his gifts and talents (1 Cor. 1:7).

5. His revelation will be the time of reward for the testings of believers (1 Peter 1:7), a time of great joy for the saints (1 Peter 4:13).

6. Creation will be delivered from the curse (Rom. 8:19).

The third word, ἐπιφάνεια, translated "manifestation" means literally "to shine upon" or "to bring forth into the light." This word is used much in Greek literature concerning the appearances of the Greek gods. The Apostle Paul uses this word in speaking of the first coming of Christ and "the grace that is now manifested by the appearing of our Saviour Jesus Christ" (2 Tim. 1:10). Six of the ten times that ἐπιφάνεια occurs in the New Testament refer to the second coming of Christ. The word clearly describes the second coming of Christ as a shining forth, or an appearance. The word is translated variously as: *appearing* (Titus 2:13), *brightness* (2 Thess. 2:8), *to give light* (Luke 1:79), *coming* (2 Tim. 1:10).

In tracing the word ἐπιφάνεια as it refers to the second coming of Christ, we learn the following facts:

1. The epiphany of Christ is used interchangeably with His parousia (2 Thess. 2:8).

2. The epiphany of Christ will bring judgment upon the Antichrist (2 Thess. 2:8).

3. His epiphany will bring in the kingdom (2 Tim. 4:1).

4. At His epiphany rewards will be given to believers (2 Tim. 4:8).

5. His epiphany will close the time of obedience and service for believers on earth (1 Tim. 6:14).

The fourth and last word, παρουσία, meaning literally "presence," refers to the second coming as objective and visible. The word is found twenty-four times in the New Testament; sixteen of these appearances refer to the second coming of Christ.

From the use of the word παρουσία in reference to the second coming of Christ, we learn the following:

1. The parousia of Christ will not be secret, but visible. It will shine as the lightning from the east to the west (Matt. 24:27).

2. The parousia of Christ will be sudden and unexpected (Matt. 24:37-39).

3. At the parousia of Christ a resurrection will take place (1 Cor. 15:23).

4. The parousia of Christ is the hope and crown of rejoicing of the believers (1 Thess. 2:19).

5. The parousia gives motivation and encouragement to Christian life and service (1 John 2:28; 2 Thess. 2:1; James 5:7, 8; 1 Thess. 3:13; 5:23).

6. The saints will be raptured at the parousia of Christ (1 Thess. 4:15).

7. The Antichrist will be judged at the parousia of Christ (2 Thess. 2:8).

8. In the last days people shall scoff at the truth of the parousia of Christ (2 Peter 3:3, 4).

### The Time of the Second Coming

The second coming of Christ will take place at the end of the great tribulation (Matt. 24:29, 30). The day and the hour of His coming is spoken of as being unknown by any man or even by angels (Matt. 24:36, 42; 25:13). A most solemn declaration is made that this time is not known "even by the Son of man" Himself. Only the Father knows the time.

Since the precise time of the second coming is unknown and since Christians are exhorted to be ready for it momentarily, the second coming of Chirst is said to be imminent. It may happen at any time. This was as true in the time of the Apostles as it is true today (James 5:8).

Even though the precise day and hour are not revealed, Christians are to discern the times and to be aware of the nearness of His coming. The end will not come until the Gospel is preached to every nation (Matt. 24:14). There will not be a complete conversion of the world, however: tares will be growing together with the wheat until the harvest (Matt. 13:30). In the last days, near the time of the harvest, the world will abound with wickedness (2 Tim. 3:1-5). However, in order that all peoples and nations may have a chance to hear the Gospel before the final harvest even under such conditions, the Lord Himself will send an angel to proclaim the Gospel to all in a supernatural way (Rev. 14:6, 7).

The day of the Lord will not come except there come the falling away first and the man of sin be revealed (2 Thess. 2:3). A great apostasy will come to pass before His return. So great is the falling away from the faith that there is even question as to whether the Son of man will find any faith on the earth when He returns (Luke 18:8).

There will also be troubles and revolutionary disturbances among the nations, and signs and distress in nature (Luke 21:25-27; Mark 13:7, 8).

### The Manner of the Second Coming

1. In personal, visible splendor, in power and glory (Acts 1:9, 11; Matt. 16:27; 26:64; Rev. 19:11-16).

2. As the lightning shines from the east to the west, not in secret (Matt. 24:26, 27; Rev. 1:7).

3. In the glory of His Father, accompanied with saints and angels (Matt. 16:27; Jude 14; 2 Thess. 1:7; Zech. 14:5; 1 Thess. 3:13; 4:14; Col. 3:4; Matt. 25:31).

4. With a shout and the voice of the archangel (1 Thess. 4:16, 17).

5. As a rider on a white horse (Rev. 19:11).

6. As a thief and as a snare (Luke 21:34, 35; 1 Thess. 5: 2, 3).

## The Purpose of the Second Coming

1. To reveal Himself with His own to be glorified in His saints (Col. 3:4; Zech. 14:5; 2 Thess. 1:10; 1 Thess 3:13).

2. To judge the beast, the antichrist, the false prophet and the armies of the earth (Rev. 19:19-21; 2 Thess. 2:8).

3. To bind Satan (Rev. 20:1, 2).

4. To save Israel as a nation (Acts 15:16; Zech. 14:3, 4; Joel 3:15, 16).

5. To judge the nations (Matt. 24:31, 32; Joel 3:1, 2, 12; 2 Thess. 1:7-9; Isa. 24:21-23).

6. To deliver and to bless creation (Rom. 8:19-22).

7. To set up His kingdom (Rev. 11:15; 20:4; Dan. 7:13, 14; Luke 21:27, 31; 2 Tim. 4:1; Zech. 14:9; Matt. 25:31).

8. To bring about a state of peace (Micah 4:3, 4; Isa. 2:4).

9. To reward the saints (Matt. 16:27; 1 Cor. 4:5; 2 Tim. 4:8; 1 Peter 5:4).

## The Christian's Attitude Toward the Second Coming

The return of Christ is the "blessed hope" of the Christian. This truth inspires the Christian to faithfulness and diligence in doing the work of God. Christ's return is an encouragement in all action and duty; and it increases the ability of the Christian to exercise a spirit of acceptance of present trials and hardships; and by the reinforcement of His presence and the assurance of His coming, it reinforces the Christian to find solutions to conflicts, where possible. The second coming is an encouragement for the following:

1. To testify and to witness for Christ (Luke 9:26);

2. To heavenly mindedness in conduct (Phil. 3:20);

3. To refrain from judging others (1 Cor. 4:5);

4. To holiness of life by loving one another (1 Thess 3:12, 13; 5:4-9);

5. To self-discipline and restraint (Luke 21:35, 36);

6. To faithfulness in service (Matt. 24:44-51; 1 Tim. 4:1, 2; 1 Cor. 1:7, 8; 1 Peter 5:1-4);

7. To patience and perseverance (Heb. 10:36-38; James 5: 7, 8);

8. To abide in Christ (1 John 2:28);

9. To put talents to use (Matt. 14:30);

10. Not to worry or to express anxiety (John 14:1-3);

11. To pray and exercise an attitude of watchfulness (Rev. 22:20);

12. To cheerfulness in bereavement (1 Thess. 4:13, 14).

### Other Views of the Second Coming

1. The second coming of Christ took place at Pentecost in the person of the Holy Spirit. Objections against this view are:

    a. The Holy Spirit is spoken of as another Comforter, and as such He is distinct from Christ (John 14:16, 17).

    b. After Pentecost the second coming of Christ is spoken of as yet future in several of the epistles (2 Thess. 2; 2 Peter 3:10) and in the book of the Revelation.

    c. Many events said to happen at the second coming of Christ did not take place at Pentecost, such as the resurrection and the battle of Armageddon.

2. The second coming of Christ took place in the fall of Jerusalem in A.D. 70. Objections against this view are:

    a. Many events said to happen at the second coming of Christ did not take place in A.D. 70 (see 1c immediately above).

b. John, who wrote the book of the Revelation about A.D. 95, was still looking for the Lord's return.

3. The second coming of Christ will be a spiritual and mystical coming in His Church. The objection against this view is the angelic prophecy that Jesus would return "in like manner" as He went (Acts 1:8).

4. The second coming of Christ would be at death. The objection to this view is that death does not happen in the manner, nor with the attending circumstances, revealed in the Scriptures. Death is an enemy; the second coming of Christ is a blessed hope. Death is abolished at His second coming (1 Cor. 15:50-57).

## Bibliography

Baines, T. B. *The Lord's Coming, Israel, and the Church.* London: Rouse, 1900.

Berkhof, Louis. *The Second Coming of Christ.* Grand Rapids, Michigan: William B. Eerdmans, 1953.

Blackstone, W. E. *Jesus Is Coming.* New York: Fleming H. Revell, 1932.

Douty, Norman F. *Has Christ's Return Two Stages?* New York: Pageant Press, 1956.

Grant, F. W. *The Revelation of Christ.* New York: Loizeaux Brothers, no date.

Gray, James M. *Prophecy and the Lord's Return.* New York: Fleming H. Revell, 1917.

————. *A Textbook on Prophecy.* New York: Fleming H. Revell, 1918.

Haldeman, I. M. *The History of the Doctrine of Our Lord's Return.* New York: First Baptist Church, no date.

Kelly, William. *Lectures on the Second Coming of the Lord Jesus Christ.* London: G. Morrish, no date.

————. *The Lord's Prophecy on Olivet in Matthew 24 and 21.* London: T. Weston, 1903.

Walvoord, John F. "New Testament Words for the Lord's Coming," *Bibliotheca Sacra,* 101:283-89 (July, 1944).

Waugh, Thomas. *When Jesus Comes.* London: Charles H. Kelly, 1901.

# TIMES OF THE GENTILES

The only biblical reference to the times of the Gentiles is Luke 21:24:

> And they shall fall by the edge of the sword, and shall be led away captive into all nations: and Jerusalem shall be trodden down of the Gentiles, until the times of the Gentiles be fulfilled.

This verse reveals that the chief characteristic of the times of the Gentiles is that Jerusalem will be under Gentile rule. This occurred first in 586 B.C., under the Babylonians, which marks the point of the setting aside of the Jews as a national witness to the things of God. Isaiah declared, however, that a remnant would be spared in order to fulfill the promises of God:

> Except the Lord of hosts had left unto us a very small remnant, we should have been as Sodom, and we should have been like unto Gomorrah (Isa. 1:9).

> But yet in it shall be a tenth, and it shall return, and shall be eaten: as a teil tree, and as an oak, whose substance is in them, when they cast their leaves: so the holy seed shall be the substance thereof (Isa. 6:13).

Micah speaks further of God's overlooking the transgressions of this remnant in order to perform the promises:

> Who is a God unto thee, that pardoneth iniquity, and passeth by the transgression of the remnant of his heritage? he retaineth not his anger for ever, because he delighteth

in mercy. He will turn again, he will have compassion upon us; he will subdue our iniquities and thou wilt cast all their sins into the depths of the sea. Thou wilt perform the truth to Jacob, and the mercy to Abraham, which thou hast sworn unto our fathers from the days of old (Micah 7:18-20).

During the times of the Gentiles, Israel will be scattered among the nations, and four great Gentile kingdoms will bear rule over Jerusalem. These four kingdoms are Babylonia, Persia, Greece, and Rome. They are represented figuratively by the:

four metals in Daniel 2
four beasts in Daniel 7
four horns in Zechariah 1:18-21
four worms in Joel 1:4; 2:25
four judgments in Ezekiel 14:21
four families in Jeremiah 15:3, 4

According to Daniel's prophecy of the seventy weeks, the times of the Gentiles, thus, could have ended during the Roman rule over Jerusalem at the time of Christ. But because of the rejection of the Messiah, the times of the Gentiles have been extended until His second coming, as Christ Himself predicted in Luke 21:24.

Three events will mark the end of the times of the Gentiles: the restoration of the Jews to Palestine; the control of the temple at Jerusalem by the Jews (Rev. 11:1, 2); and the completion of God's purpose among the Gentiles (Rom. 11:25-27).

Sing, O daughter of Zion; shout, O Israel; be glad and rejoice with all thy heart, O daughter of Jerusalem. The Lord hath taken away thy judgments, he hath cast out thine enemy: the king of Israel, even the Lord, is in the midst of thee: thou shalt not see evil any more. . . . At that time will I bring you again, even in the time that I gather you: for I will make you a name and a praise among all people of the earth, when I turn back your captivity before your eyes, saith the Lord (Zeph. 3:14, 15, 20).

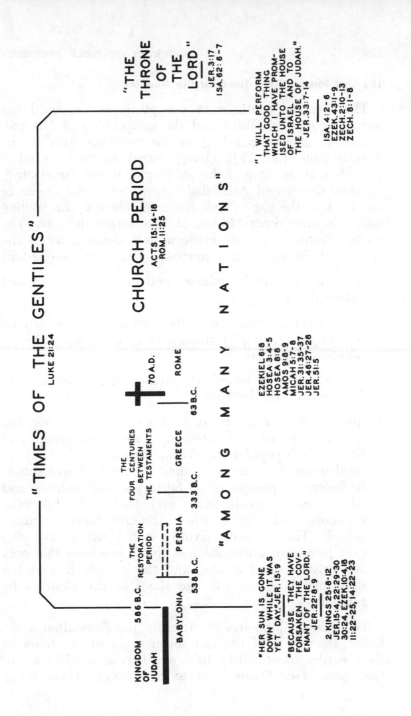

"TIMES OF THE GENTILES"
LUKE 21:24

"THE THRONE OF THE LORD"
JER.3:17
ISA.62:6-7

KINGDOM OF JUDAH

586 B.C.

BABYLONIA

538 B.C.

THE RESTORATION PERIOD

PERSIA

333 B.C.

GREECE

THE FOUR CENTURIES BETWEEN THE TESTAMENTS

63 B.C.

ROME

70 A.D.

CHURCH PERIOD
ACTS 15:14-18
ROM.11:25

"AMONG MANY NATIONS"

"HER SUN IS GONE DOWN WHILE IT WAS YET DAY."JER.15:9

"BECAUSE THEY HAVE FORSAKEN THE COVENANT OF THE LORD."
JER.22:8-9

2 KINGS 25:8-12
JER.15:4,22:29-30
30:24,EZEK.10:4,18
11:22-25,14:22-23

EZEKIEL 6:8
HOSEA 3:4-5
HOSEA 8:8
AMOS 9:8-9
MICAH 5:7-8
JER.31:35-37
JER.46:27-28
JER.5:5

"I WILL PERFORM THAT GOOD THING WHICH I HAVE PROMISED UNTO THE HOUSE OF ISRAEL AND TO THE HOUSE OF JUDAH."
JER.33:7-14

ISA.4:2-6
EZEK.43:1-9
ZECH.2:10-13
ZECH.8:1-8

### The Last Phase of the Times of the Gentiles

The Gentiles continue to occupy Jerusalem until the second coming of Christ and the establishing of His millennial kingdom, according to the prophecy also of the Apostle John (Rev. 11). Though Israel obtained control of Jerusalem at the time of the Six Day War, not Israel's flag, but any designated Arab flag may fly over the Dome of the Rock — the site of Solomon's temple and the wailing wall — or over other Moslem shrines within the city. The United Nations has not made a final decision as to the control of the city. Four proposals have been suggested:

1. A return to the boundaries and controls that existed before the Six Day War;

2. Internationalization under the controls of the United Nations, either of all Jerusalem or of those sections with religious significance;

3. Formalization of Israel's *de facto* control over the Old City as well as the New.

4. Authorization of Israel's control over the entire city, but with some measure of autonomy for religious groups and for the Arab population. Washington contends: (1) Jerusalem should remain a united city; (2) There should be access for persons of all faiths and nationalities; and (3) Roles for both Israel and Jordan in the civic, economic, and religious life of the city should be maintained. This carefully avoids saying whose flag flies over Jerusalem, and reinforces John's prophecy that only at Christ's second coming and the inauguration of His millennial kingdom will the times of the Gentiles be fulfilled.

The Apostle John has recorded in the Revelation a detailed description of the last seven years of the times of the Gentiles, identified by Bible teachers as Daniel's seventieth week (see DANIEL'S SEVENTY WEEKS). These seven years will be characterized by conquest, war, famine, persecution of Christians, death, and hell. The Antichrist, supported by the false prophet of the end times, will rule the kingdoms of the earth with a confederacy of ten kings (Rev. 17:11-18).

The last three and a half years of this tribulation period at the end of the age are especially noted by John as an unparalleled time of trouble (Rev. 11:2, 3; 12:6, 14; 13:5; cf. Dan. 12:6, 7). During this time God will extend a final invitation to the nations to repent (Rev. 14:6; 11:3-11), but they will not repent (Rev. 9:21; 16:9, 21); and the judgments of God will pour forth over the earth to a limited extent of one-third destruction at first (Rev. 8:7-12). But with the continued rejection of God by the nations the final judgments — the undiluted wrath of God — will bring total destruction (Rev. 15 and 16). In fury the Antichrist gathers the armies of his confederacy at Armageddon to fight against the Lamb, and he and his allies are destroyed by the brightness of Christ's second coming (Rev. 19:11-21; cf. 2 Thess. 2:8). And thus ends the "times of the Gentiles."

# THE GREAT TRIBULATION

### Definition

The word "tribulation" means "to press" (as grapes), "to press together," "to press hard upon," and refers to times of oppression, affliction, and distress (Thayer). The word is translated variously as "tribulation," "affliction," "anguish," "persecution," "trouble," "burden." It is used to describe the state of:

1. Those hard pressed by siege and calamities of war (Matt. 24:21, 29; Mark 13:19, 24);

2. Those pressed by want and poverty (2 Cor. 8:13; Phil. 4:14);

3. A woman in child-birth (John 16:21);

4. Afflictions Christ had to undergo (and from which His followers must not shrink) (Col. 1:24);

5. Anxiety, burden of heart (2 Cor. 2:4);

6. A period of tribulation out of which a great multitude will be saved (Rev. 7:14).

Christ used the word to describe the way which leads to life, saying: "Strait is the gate and narrow (tributory) is the way" (Matt. 7:14). Christ also said that tribulation and persecution may come because of obedience to the Gospel (Matt. 13:21). He told the disciples that they would have tribulation; they would be afflicted (tribulated) and

184

even killed for His name's sake (Matt. 24:9). Nevertheless, they should be of good cheer, He encouraged, for He had overcome the world (John 16:33).

The Apostle Paul told the Corinthians that when he was in affliction (tribulation), it was for their sakes (2 Cor. 1: 16). Paul also said that he and his associates suffered trouble (tribulation) on every side (2 Cor. 4:8) by fightings without and fears within (2 Cor. 7:5). He told the Thessalonians that they would suffer tribulation (1 Thess. 3:4), but that they would receive rest from their tribulation when the Lord Jesus would be revealed from heaven. At that time Christ would recompense tribulation on those who troubled the Thessalonians (2 Thess. 1:6, 7). Paul told the Romans that he gloried in tribulation, knowing that it brought patience (Rom. 5:3). Tribulation could not separate from Christ's love (Rom. 8:35). Paul was comforted by God in the midst of his tribulation (2 Cor. 1:4) and could thereby comfort others in their tribulation with the same comfort that he received. Nor was his tribulation light, for he was "pressed out of measure, above strength," so much that he "despaired even of life" (2 Cor. 1:8). Nevertheless, he was exceedingly joyful in all tribulation (2 Cor. 7:4), counting it as a light thing which was but for a moment, but which, obtained for him a far more exceeding and eternal weight of glory (2 Cor. 4:17). He exhorted his converts to continue in the faith, telling them that they must through much tribulation enter into the kingdom of God (Acts 14:22).

The Apostle John said that he was a brother and companion in tribulation with the faithful of Asia Minor (Rev. 1:9). Other appearances of the word as used by John in the book of Revelation are in chapters 2:9, 10, 22 and 7:14. The last reference, referring to "the great tribulation," will be taken up in detail below.

These twenty-six appearances of the word "tribulation" may be said to be representative of its fifty-four occurrences in the New Testament.

## The Great Tribulation

1. A definite period of time at the end of the age immediately preceding the Lord's return to earth (Matt. 24: 29-35; Mark 13).

2. Known as "the tribulation — the great one" (Rev. 7:14), out of which are saved a great multitude of all nations, kindreds, people, and tongues.

3. Of such severity that no period in history past or future will equal it (Matt. 24:21).

4. A shortened period for the elect's sake (Matt. 24:22) else no flesh could stand it.

5. The time referred to in Scripture as Jacob's trouble, a judgment upon God-rejecting nation and upon Messiah-rejecting Israel (Jer. 30:7; Dan. 12:1-4; Matt. 24:15).

6. A time of judgment upon the nations for their sin and rejection of Christ (Isa. 26:21; 27; 34:1, 2; Rev. 6:15-17).

7. Of seven years duration, the length of Daniel's seventieth week (see DANIEL'S SEVENTIETH WEEK).

Bible teachers differ as to the nature and extent of "the great tribulation." Some identify the phrase "the great tribulation" with "the wrath of God." These would interpret the seals, the trumpets, and the bowls of the Revelation as outpourings of God's wrath. On the basis of this interpretation, they affirm the rapture of the Church to be *before* the opening of the first seal and "the great tribulation" to concern only the unbelieving nations, Gentiles and Jews alike.

Others interpret the phrase, "the great tribulation," to refer to troublesome times that both the Church and unbelievers shall experience at the end times. These differentiate between the seals and trumpets, on the one hand, and the bowls of God's undiluted wrath, on the other. The seals and trumpets, they affirm, refer to suffering caused by the wrath of man, which God uses to encourage men to repent. The bowls, however, are especially designated as the fullness of the wrath of God. On the basis of this interpretation, they affirm that the rapture of the Church takes place *after* the opening of the seals and the blowing of the trumpets, but immediately *before* the pouring out of the seven bowls of wrath. Those who interpret the time of the seven bowls as in the middle of the seven last years are known as mid-tribulationists. Those who affirm that the bowls are poured out, one immediately after another in rapid succession at the end of the time and of the end are known as post-tribulationists.

# APPENDIX:

# Creative Ideas and Questions
# on
# Bible Prophecy

The following creative ideas for Bible study classes have been added to increase the effective use of *A Survey of Bible Prophecy* in four different areas:

1. *INDEPENDENT STUDY QUESTIONS:* for the individual who wants to advance his knowledge either privately at home or under supervision in a Bible class in a secondary institution.

2. *RESEARCH PAPER SUGGESTIONS:* for the extra-heavy, scholarly home Bible study classes and for the academic classroom.

3. *CREATIVE PROJECTS:* for Bible classes in Christian secondary institutions or in advanced and innovative Sunday schools.

4. *GROUP DISCUSSION:* for all those Christians who wish to make the prophecies of the end times relevant to their present affective experience.

# APPENDIX

## ANTICHRIST

### INDEPENDENT STUDY QUESTIONS

#### Biblical Use of Word

1. In what two ways is the word "Antichrist" used in the New Testament? 1 John 2:18,22; 4:3; 2 John 7

2. Is the word "Antichrist" ever used to refer to the great opponent of Christ in the end times? What names are given to this anti-Christian world leader? Daniel 7:7; 9:26; 2 Thessalonians 2:8; Revelation 11:7; 13:1-10

#### Time of His Coming

3. What events must happen before the Antichrist of the end times appears? 2 Thessalonians 2:1-3

4. How long does he rule? Daniel 9:27; Revelation 11:2,3; 12:6,14; 13:5

5. What events mark the end of his rule? Revelation 6:12-17; 11:15-19; 17:12-14; 19:11-20; 2 Thessalonians 2:8; Daniel 7:24-27

#### Political and Religious Operations

6. What will be his relationship *politically* to Israel? Daniel 7:25; 9:27; 12:7. To other government heads ruling at the same time? Revelation 17:8-14; 19:19; Daniel 7:23,24

7. How does he gain control? 2 Thessalonians 2:9-12; Revelation 13:11-17

8. What will be his relationship *religiously* to Israel? Daniel 9:27; 12:1; Revelation 12:13-17. To all believers? Revelation 7:14; 6:9-11; 13:5-17; 16:6; 17:6; Daniel 7:21

9. How will God protect believers? Daniel 12:1,2; Revelation 7; 12:7

## Goals of Antichrist

10. At what ultimate targets are the Antichrist's activities directed? Name at least three. Revelation 13:6,7,15-17; 17:12-14; 19:19; Daniel 7:25; 12:7 (cf. Rev. 12:13)

## His End

11. What will be the end of the Antichrist and his kingdom? Daniel 7:26,27; Revelation 19:19; 20:10; 2 Thessalonians 2:8

## RESEARCH PAPERS

1. The function of Michael the archangel in the events of the end times (see Dan. 12 and Rev. 12).

2. An interpretation of Daniel 11:36-45.

3. Identification of the second beast of Revelation 13: various views.

4. Characteristics and behavior of the Antichrist of the end times.

5. The politics of the Antichrist.

6. Relation of the Antichrist to believers.

## CREATIVE PROJECTS

1. Dramatic dialogue. Three people living during the last three and one-half years of the end times are discussing current events. Write a dialogue of their conversation.

2. Dramatic monologue. Using stream-of-consciousness style of writing, explore the motivations and thoughts of one of the following:

    a. the Antichrist of the end times

    b. one of the 144,000 sealed Israelites (see Rev. 7:3-8; 14:1-5)

    c. one of the two witnesses preaching the Gospel in Jerusalem during the last 3½ years (see Rev. 11:1-13)

3. Create a television news report (with accompanying on-the-scene action film), announcing the death of the two witnesses of the end times, killed by Antichrist, and the resultant festivity over the world.

4. In one column, every member of the class writes *ten half-sentences*. They switch papers, and in the second column, they complete correctly the second half. For example:

    The attitude of the Antichrist toward believers is _____.

The several groups of witnesses to God's truth in the end times are

_____

_____.

The confederates of Antichrist are _____,

5. Preparation of a bibliography and/or an oral review of one of the current books on Satan.

6. Prepare a chart of Antichrist's activities in the end times.

## GROUP DISCUSSION

In what ways might a Christian slip into "anti-Christian" attitudes and actions? How do Christians sometimes "persecute" other believers, as the Antichrist of the end times will — in social groups, in business, in the home, in school?

# ARMAGEDDON

## INDEPENDENT STUDY QUESTIONS

### Participants

1. From what places do the participants of Armageddon come? Revelation 16:12-16; Joel 3:2; Zechariah 14:1,2; 12:3

### Purpose

2. For what purpose? Zechariah 14:2

### Time

3. At what time? Revelation 16:12-16; Zechariah 14:1-4; Joel 3:1,15,16

### Place

4. What other name is given to this battle of the end times? Joel 3:2,12,14

### Result

5. What great event climaxes the battle of Armageddon? Revelation 19:19-21; Joel 3:12-14

6. What happens to the participants? Revelation 19:15-20

## RESEARCH PAPERS

1. The topography of Armageddon, the military strategy of past generals engaging in war in that place, and the victories and defeats of participating armies.

2. The arguments for/against identification of the battle of Armageddon with the Gog and Magog invasion, as some Bible scholars teach.

## CREATIVE PROJECTS

1. Write a short beast fable on Armageddon with the various animals of the world planning strategies and arming themselves against their Creator.

2. Conduct an imaginative committee meeting of armament makers of the end times, the president of a company and his executive advisers sitting in the president's conference room around a table.

3. Map out military maneuvers of various participating armies on a map.

4. Write a dialogue between a hawk and a raven as they eat the carnage of the battlefield.

5. Write a ballad about a wife and mother, widowed by the Armageddon struggle.

## GROUP DISCUSSION

1. Describe the feelings of a soldier who hesitates because he is not fully persuaded of his general's purpose in preparing for Armageddon. The soldier finally repents as Christ breaks through the heavens.

2. How would you feel if the company for which you worked practiced immoral activities? What would you do?

# BABYLON

## INDEPENDENT STUDY QUESTIONS

### Its Identification

1. What passages of Scripture suggest Babylon as a literal commercial city of the end times? Revelation 18:10-19

2. What passages suggest it as the capital of Antichrist? Revelation 17:3,7,8,18

3. What passages have been interpreted as suggestive of a religious affiliation, some system or institution of wickedness, in the end times? Revelation 17:5,6; 18:2-5,23,24

## Its Restoration

4. Give the two main arguments for the restoration of a *literal* city in the Near East. Jeremiah 25:17-26,30-33; Isaiah 13:19,20

5. The chief argument against a literal restoration rests on a symbolic interpretation of prophetic passages on Babylon. Explain. Zechariah 5:5-11; Revelation 17:5

## Persons and Events

6. Name at least five people or groups connected with Babylon of the end times. Revelation 17 and 18

7. List at least five events that take place in the city. Revelation 17 and 18

8. What warning is given to believers against Babylon's influence? Revelation 14:8-13; 18:4,5

## Its Fall

9. How does the fall of Babylon take place? Revelation 17:15-18

10. What climactic events immediately follow her fall? Revelation 14:14,15,17-19; 19:1-21

## RESEARCH PAPERS

1. Arguments for/against a restored Babylon.

2. An inquiry into the interpretation of Babylon as Rome.

3. An interpretation of the seven heads and ten horns of the beast on which Mystery Babylon sits.

4. A history and description of archaeological artifacts that demonstrate ancient Babylon's complete overthrow.

## CREATIVE PROJECTS

1. Draw an architect's design of a new Tower of Babel or the Hanging Gardens as possible tourist attractions in a restored Babylon.

2. Write an imaginative dialogue between two bricks bearing the old

Babylon stamp, being carried away from Babylon by invaders to help build a house in Baghdad, or Seleucia, or Ctesiphon, or al Maiden, or Kufa (cities built with bricks from Babylon).

3. Create a discussion between several Israelites in captivity in Babylon, who have just read Jeremiah's prophecies about Babylon. Jeremiah 25:17-26,30-33; 50:3,8,39,40; 51:6,26,43,45

4. Fantasize what Daniel or Ezekiel (both were prophets in the Babylonian Captivity of the Old Testament times) would say if he could reappear invisibly and walk the streets of the wicked city of the end times.

5. Prepare a trade journal or newspaper or travel tour advertising the Babylon of the end times, its tourist attractions, and its crafts and products (see *Americana Encyclopedia*, 1972, "Iraq").

6. Create a "Peanuts" cartoon series as it might appear in a Babylon newspaper, analytical and critical of the culture, but also assertive in lessons of faith, hope, charity, and other virtues.

## GROUP DISCUSSION

Obviously, in the end times conformity will characterize the attitudes and actions of most people. When should a person conform? When should he resist? Who are usually responsible for human progress — people who try to be exactly like everyone else or people who dare to be somewhat "different"? What is your evidence? May "different-ness" be carried too far? What is the relation of the "different" members of the Body of Christ to the harmonious unity of the whole?

# THE CHURCH

## INDEPENDENT STUDY QUESTIONS

### Description/Definition

1. How is the word "church" used in the New Testament? Acts 2:47; Ephesians 5:27; 1 Corinthians 12:18; Acts 8:1; Romans 16:5; 1 Corinthians 11:18; 14:19,28

2. Give ten synonyms or descriptive epithets used of the Church in the New Testament. 1 Peter 2:5; Ephesians 2:21,22; 5:27; 1:23; 1 Corinthians 12:27; 1 Timothy 3:15; Hebrews 12:23; 1 Corinthians 10:32; 14:33; Galatians 1:13

## Organization

3. How does a person become a member? Acts 2:47; Ephesians 5:25; Matthew 16:16-18; Acts 2:38-41

4. Describe its organization. Ephesians 2:20,21; 1 Corinthians 12:12; Matthew 16:18; Acts 6:2-6; 14:23; 1 Timothy 3

5. What are its ordinances? Matthew 28:19,20; Acts 2:42,46. What does "ordinance" mean?

6. Describe its calling and destiny. Colossians 3:1,2; Ephesians 1:4,6; 4:13; Acts 1:8; 1 Thessalonians 4:16,17

## Relation to Israel

7. What is the Church's relation to Israel? Romans 11:12-26. What verses in this passage suggest a national repentance on the part of Israel? What Old Testament verse suggests similarly a national repentance? Zechariah 12:10. What does this verse add?

8. What references are cited by those who would say that Israel as a nation is absorbed into a spiritual Israel, i.e., the Church? Galatians 3:7,14,28,29; Romans 2:28,29; 3:29,30; 4:16,17

9. What difference does this view make in the interpretation of Revelation 12?

## RESEARCH PAPERS

1. Relation of Jew and Gentile in the Old Testament.

2. Israel in the end times.

3. The history of the Promise (Redeemer) in the Old Testament.

4. Principles of church government in various denominations.

5. Relation of the Church to the Old Testament Law.

## CREATIVE PROJECTS

1. Draw charts demonstrating patterns of church government of various denominations.

2. Fold an 8½ x 11 sheet of paper lengthwise. On one side list all Old Testament prophecies to Israel. On the other side list how they might be interpreted by those who would spiritualize Israel into the Church in the New Testament.

3. Panel discussion on church discipline. Pros and cons.

4. Describe the sacraments of the Roman Catholic Church with the ordinances of the Protestant. Explain the rationale behind the difference.

5. Write a paper on the different ways of celebrating ordinances, such as sprinkling or immersing for the ordinance of baptism. Include in your study unique activities that accompany the celebration of ordinances, such as foot-washing.

## GROUP DISCUSSION

Assign in advance to several different class members the following: Give oral reports on "Your Church and Its Affiliation(s)," its origin, history, organization, unique doctrinal emphasis, outreach, discipline, missions, relation of the local church to the national organization and to other denominations.

# DANIEL'S SEVENTY WEEKS

## INDEPENDENT STUDY QUESTIONS

### Historical Background

1. Why did Daniel pray for more light on the duration of the Babylonian Captivity? Daniel 9:2,21-27; Jeremiah 25:11

### Divisions

2. Why are the Seventy Weeks broken into sixty-nine and one week? Daniel 9:25,26

3. What text supports the interpretation of the weeks as "weeks of years," i.e., seventy times seven years? Daniel 9:25,26

### Time

4. What marks the beginning of the seventieth and last week? What marks the middle of the week? What change in the behavior of the "prince" marks the two halves of the seventieth week as different from each other? Daniel 9:25-27

5. Why is the seventieth week thought to be postponed to the time of the end? Daniel 9:24,27

6. What other passages of Scripture relate to the last half of the week

or three and a half years? Daniel 12:1,12; Revelation 12:6,14; 13:5; 11:2,3

7. What events take place during this time (same references as question #6)?

## RESEARCH PAPERS

1. Events of the last half of Daniel's seventieth week.
2. Inquiry into the Postponement Theory.
3. Relation of Israel to the seventieth week.
4. Interpretation of "the Abomination of Desolation."

## CREATIVE PROJECTS

1. Write a brief drama on Daniel's meditations on Jeremiah's prophecy, the coming of the angel to answer his prayer, the layout of the prophetic calendar, and Daniel's response.

2. Prepare a *mathematical* chart on the seventy-sevens of years, taking into account leap years, leap centuries, 360-day year of the O.T., etc.

3. Prepare a *historical* and *chronological* chart of the events of the seventy weeks.

4. Write a dramatic monologue on a character whose friend has betrayed his trust, as the "prince" of the end times betrays the trust of Israel.

5. Write a stream-of-consciousness soliloquy of the "prince" who breaks the covenant with Israel.

6. Imaginative projective. What will be some of the major problems of Israel during the seventieth week?

## GROUP DISCUSSION

As the "prince" of the end times breaks a covenant and betrays those who trusted him, so also do some persons now prove disloyal to their "friends" and betray their trust. What outside circumstances in a person's life provide a climate congenial to his becoming a traitor to his friends? Is he entirely responsible for what happens? Are there any times when a person is justified in breaking a pledge? If so, when and how?

# EZEKIEL'S MILLENNIAL GEOGRAPHY

## INDEPENDENT STUDY QUESTIONS

### Historical Background

1. Where was Ezekiel living when he received the visions of the restoration of the temple, of the sacrificial offerings, and of the land? What difference does it make whether Ezekiel 40-48 should be taken literally or figuratively?

### Restoration of the Temple

2. How would a person go about discovering whether Ezekiel's visions have reference to the temple built when some captive Israelites returned from Babylon to Palestine?

3. Suppose the temple of this prophecy is really built and the sacrifices reinstituted during the millennium, what might be the relationship of this ancient worship to Christ who will be the ruling Prince at the time? Isaiah 2:3,4; Zechariah 14:16-21

### Principles of Interpretation

4. One of the major objections to the restoration of a millennial temple is the prophetic description of the "prince," a description that could not refer to Christ. Why not? What is the nature of these prophecies? Ezekiel 45:7-10,16-18,22

5. Cite the New Testament references which support a symbolic interpretation of the temple, sacrifices, and land. 1 Corinthians 3:16; 2 Corinthians 6:16; Revelation 3:12; 7:15; 21:22; Romans 12:1; 15:16; Philippians 2:17; 4:18; 1 Peter 2:5,9; Hebrews 13:15

## RESEARCH PAPERS

1. Comparison of the dimensions given for Ezekiel's temple with those of Solomon's temple and of the restoration temple.

2. Amillennial interpretations of Ezekiel 40-48.

3. The prince and the people connected with Ezekiel's temple.

4. Hermeneutical principles involved in the interpretation of Ezekiel 40-48.

5. The twelve tribes of Israel in relation to Ezekiel's prophecy.

## CREATIVE PROJECTS

1. Build a scale model of Ezekiel's temple.

2. Make a year calendar listing the days for each sacrifice and feast.

3. Fold an 8½ x 11 sheet of paper lengthwise into two columns. Above one column write VALUES and above the other write TABOOS. Then list what is valued and what is not valued in Ezekiel 40-48.

4. Write or conduct an antiphony to celebrate the restoration of a destroyed temple, using various groups to comment: those who shout for joy over its restoration; those who weep because they have seen it better; those who stand by in limbo, not making up their minds (see Ezra 3:10-13).

5. Study Leviticus and Deuteronomy for facts about ancient Israelitish festivals and holidays. Compare with modern celebrations. Prepare skits presenting both the ancient and the modern ways of celebration.

6. Write a sonnet on the believer as the "temple" in which the Spirit of God dwells. 1 Corinthians 3:16; 2 Corinthians 6:15; Revelation 3:12; 7:15; 21:22

## GROUP DISCUSSION

The ceremonial laws of the Old Testament were given to remind Israel of the Promise of the Redeemer to come in the seed of Abraham and of their need of Him. For instance, for Israelites to be required to ask themselves at meal times, "Is this food kosher?" became a continual reminder that they were a people especially separated by God as bearers of the Promise. When a hawk flew overhead, or a rabbit ran across their path, any unclean bird or animal, they were reminded of their special mission as a separated people. What sort of reminder do you have to recall you to God? Should you develop more reminders? What kind?

# GOG AND MAGOG

Questions are included under the section on MILLENNIUM.

# JUDGMENTS

## INDEPENDENT STUDY QUESTIONS
### Personal

1. Who are judged at "the first resurrection"? Who are judged at "the

great white throne"? Revelation 20:4,5,12

## Rewards

2. Describe the rewards given to believers. 1 Corinthians 3:11-15; 9:25; 2 Timothy 4:8; James 1:12; 1 Peter 5:4; Revelation 2:10

3. What arguments can be given for interpreting the "crowns" as symbolic of entrance into eternity rather than as literal headpieces?

4. When does the judgment of believers take place? Matthew 19:28; 1 Corinthians 6:2,3; 2 Corinthians 5:10; Revelation 20:4,5

## Punishments

5. What is the time relationship between the millennium and the judgment of the wicked dead? Revelation 20:5,12

6. When will the Antichrist and his followers be judged? Revelation 19:20; 20:10

7. What is the chief principle of judgment? Romans 2:12-16

## RESEARCH PAPERS

1. The judgment seat of Christ.
2. The justice of divine judgment.
3. God's judgments in the Old Testament.
4. Is capital punishment justifiable according to the Bible?
5. Relationship of love and justice.
6. God's use of judgment in history (see, for instance, the punishment of Israel and the nations in the Old Testament, and the trumpets and vials of Revelation 8,9,15-16).

## CREATIVE PROJECTS

1. Role-play a court scene in which a lawyer is pleading that his client (who is guilty of murder) be pardoned.
2. List all the factors involved in making a valid judgment statement. What factors did God think were valid in judging Israel in the Old Testament?
3. Conflict-resolution practice. Role-play the following difficult situ-

ations to acquire skill in controlling the situation and in keeping your actions consonant with your values:

a. Set time limits on work to be done by your employee/children who have become delinquent in their performance.

b. Interpret your new function as coach of a boys' baseball team. Encourage and inspire them when they have just lost a game which you felt they could have won.

c. Control a mischievous roommate/brother/sister who has been excessively playing tricks on you, filling the room from floor to ceiling with crumpled newspapers, spraying the room with perfume, short-sheeting your bed or putting stones, frogs, or lizards in it, making dates for you on the phone with the opposite sex by faking your voice and using your name, etc.

d. Explain your position as newly appointed chief of an office force or organization in which the former chief is yet a member. He has been deposed because of inefficiency.

e. Quiet an incessant talker in a meeting or organization of which you are chairman or president.

f. Announce the failure of an organization which you initiated to your best friend/husband/wife who greatly admires you.

g. The other party on your telephone line has been talking for half an hour while you've been trying to get a doctor for your child. Tell him you need the phone.

4. Panel discussion on the nature of truth. Do we have truth? What is the nature of truth, subjective/objective, relative/absolute? What is the relation of the believer to truth? the unbeliever? Is the unbeliever responsible for knowing truth? Romans 1 and 2; John 1; 1 John 1

5. Fold your paper lengthwise. In one column list every kind of thought or action that is commended in *one* of the books of the Bible (your choice!) and in the other column list everything which is judged in that book.

## GROUP DISCUSSION

An encounter with judgments/decisions. Each one writes down as many factors involved in making judgments/decisions as he can provide.

Then the group divides into smaller units of three each. Members of the smaller groups share their lists with each other for ten minutes.

The leader then asks for volunteers from the separate groups to share what they have discussed. To stimulate discussion, such questions as listed in #4 of CREATIVE PROJECTS may be used.

# KINGDOM

## INDEPENDENT STUDY QUESTIONS

### Characteristics

1. What characterizes the kingdom which God will set up in the end? 1 Chronicles 17:11,14; Daniel 2:44; 7:14,18,22; Psalm 45:6; Revelation 20:1-10

2. What characterizes those who "enter" the kingdom? Matthew 5:3,10,19; 7:21; 17:3,4; 19:14,23,24; Mark 9:1,47; 10:14,15,23-25; Luke 7:28; 9:62; 18:17,24,25,29; John 3:3-5; Acts 14:22 (cf. Rom. 5:3); 1 Corinthians 6:9,10; 15:50; Galatians 5:21

3. What textual support is there for interpreting the phrases "kingdom of heaven" and "kingdom of God" as interchangeable? (See especially footnotes on the translation of Acts 20:25.)

### Alternate Interpretations

4. Which texts support the "kingdom" as a spiritual attitude of the believer? Luke 17:21; Romans 14:17; 1 Corinthians 4:20

5. Which texts add that the "kingdom" is also a *literal* one yet to come? Mark 14:25; Luke 19:11; 21:31; 22:16,18; Revelation 12:10

6. What is the "postponement theory"? What does this theory say about Christ's offer of a kingdom to Israel? Matthew 11:20-30; 12:14-21; 21:4,5; Zechariah 9:9; John 6:66; 18:39,40. In this view, which phrase is the more inclusive: "kingdom of God" or "kingdom of heaven"? How is the following question answered by this view: "If Christ's offer of a kingdom had been accepted by Israel, how then could He become the rejected, crucified Redeemer of the world?"

7. Give at least three supports to the view that Christ had no intention of setting up an earthly kingdom at His first coming, but only at His Second Coming — a view contrary to the "postponement theory." Matthew 25:31; Romans 14:17; John 3:3,5; 18:36; Colossians 1:13; Luke 19:12-15; 2 Timothy 4:1. How does this view understand the phrases "kingdom of heaven" and "kingdom of God"?

## RESEARCH PAPERS

1. Comparative study of "the kingdom of God" and the "kingdom of heaven."

2. Proponents of the Postponement Theory and their basic tenets.

3. Nature of the kingdom "within you" (see Luke 17:21).

4. Time of the coming of His kingdom.

5. A study of a utopian community (see #5 of CREATIVE PROJECTS).

## CREATIVE PROJECTS

1. Plan a festival celebrating some utopian society in history — Oneida Community, house of David, Amana Colony, Huguenots, Mennonites, Zion, etc. Prepare dress and food like theirs; present a slide show of extant pictures or art of the group; display artifacts (or re-create some) which were/are produced by the group; read/display selections of literature written by the group. Invite other classes to an evening festival with the class.

2. Prepare a montage of pictures which expresses your dream of a utopia.

3. Contrast the Antichrist's kingdom with Christ's.

4. Panel discussion on plans for several utopias written in the past: More's *Utopia*; Butler's *Erewhon*; Wells' *A Modern Utopia*, etc. Donald Gray and Allan Orrick's *Designs of Famous Utopias* (Holt, Rinehart and Winston; Arno Press, New York) also has a collection of forty-one reprints on utopian literature.

5. Write a paper on freedom and/or conformity in a utopian society. You might want to consider negative utopias like Wells' *1984* or Ionesco's *Rhinoceros*.

6. Utopian Surprise Box. What would you want in a Utopian Surprise Box for your parents? Your brothers and sisters? Your relatives? Your best friend? What would you want for poor people? What is the biggest thing you'd like? The smallest?

7. Write a one-scene drama on one of the utopian communities. Suggestion: Teenager questions the necessity of conforming to the cultural patterns of the community.

## GROUP DISCUSSION

1. T. S. Eliot has said that man cannot stand too much well-being.

Others have noted that — no matter how idyllic the achievements — every generation cleanses itself of the preceding generation either by a bloody or a bloodless revolution. Discuss your response to T. S. Eliot's statement with the group.

2. Fantasize. Create a utopian kingdom in which all of your dreams would be realized. How long would you want it to last? Who would be your friends? What kind of food, clothing, shelter, entertainment would you want? What place would children and old people have? What about wild animals?

3. In using the Lord's Prayer, we all pray, "Thy kingdom come." Discuss and share the following questions and your response:

a. Would I want God's kingdom to come this very minute? Would my plans be interrupted? How do my plans and His kingdom relate?

b. The Bible says that we are "co-laborers" with God. What is my share in preparing the way for His kingdom to come?

c. Do I now practice the commandments and rules of His kingdom as revealed in the Bible?

d. Do I harbor a worldly idol as a co-regent in my heart?

e. What is my real, unmasked interest in His kingdom, in my trust in God, in my self-surrender to God?

f. In what state are the virtues which I am supposed to exercise?

g. Am I like John the Baptist, eagerly trying to prepare other people's hearts for the coming of the kingdom: "Repent for the kingdom of heaven is at hand"?

h. Do I really "long" for the coming of His kingdom? Do I hunger and thirst for success — in His kingdom?

i. Does Christ already rule in all the departments of my soul? Am I motivated and charged by the "kingdom within"? Are there any areas of my soul still under the rule of the world, the ego, and the devil?

## THE LAST TIMES

### INDEPENDENT STUDY QUESTIONS

Matthew 24 — Mark 13 — Luke 21

These chapters present the reply of Jesus to His disciples' questions:

"What shall be the sign of thy coming? and of the end of the world?"

## False Prophets

1. What message will the false persuaders of the end times deliver? Matthew 24:4,5,11,23-25; Luke 21:8

2. How can such false persuaders be recognized? 1 John 4:1-3; 1 Timothy 4:1-3

3. What will be their end? Mark 13:21-23

## Wars and Rumors of Wars

4. What attitude should the believer have toward wars? Matthew 24:6,7; Mark 13:7,8; Luke 21:9-11

5. What is the time relationship between wars and the time of the end? Matthew 24:6; Mark 13:7; Luke 21:9

6. What natural consequences follow the wars? Matthew 24:7; Mark 13:8; Luke 21:11; Revelation 6:4-8

## Persecution and Tribulation

7. Who will be persecuted? Matthew 24:9,10; Mark 13:9-13; Luke 21:12-17

8. Why? (same references as #7 and also Revelation 6:9-11)

9. What should be the attitude of those who are persecuted? Matthew 24:13; Mark 13:9,11,13; Luke 21:13-15,19; Revelation 13:9,10,18

## Blasphemy Against God

10. To what does "the abomination of desolation" (Matt. 24:15; Mark 13:14) refer? Daniel 9:27; 2 Thessalonians 2:3,4; Revelation 13:5-8; 14; 15

11. This prophecy was fulfilled partially in the fall of Jerusalem in A.D. 70 (Matt. 24:15-20). How do we know that its complete fulfillment is in the end times? Matthew 24:21,29,30; Mark 13:19,24-27; Daniel 12:1-13

## Signs in the Heavens

12. What signs in the heavens precede Christ's return? Matthew 24:29; Mark 13:24-26; Luke 21:25-28; Revelation 6:12-14; 8:12; 19:11

13. What effect do these signs have on unbelievers? Revelation 6:15-17; 9:20,21; Matthew 24:33,42-51; Mark 13:29-37; Luke 21:28,34-36

## Christ's Return

14. How many people will see Christ return? Matthew 24:27,28,30

15. How will the unrepentant receive Him? Matthew 24:30; Luke 21:26; Revelation 6:16,17; 17:14; 19:19

16. What role do the angels have at His coming? Matthew 24:31; Mark 13:27; Revelation 14:14-20

17. Describe the three angelic announcements accompanying His coming given in Revelation 14: (1) Revelation 14:6,7; (2) Revelation 14:8; (3) Revelation 14:9

18. Who knows the precise time of His return? Matthew 24:36,42,44; Mark 13:32,35.

19. How much time does it take? Matthew 24:27; Mark 13:35,36; 1 Thessalonians 5:2; 1 Corinthians 15:52; Revelation 14:14-16

## The Human Condition

20. What characterizes those living at the end times? In general? Matthew 24:37,38; 2 Timothy 3:1-5. In regard to faith in God? Luke 18:8; 1 Timothy 4:1-3; 2 Timothy 4:3,4; 2 Peter 3:3,4

## RESEARCH PAPERS

1. Write a paper on the role of angels in the end times. Daniel 12; Revelation 12; Revelation 7:1-3; 8:2-13; 9:1,13-15; 10:1-11; 12:7-9; 14:6-9,15-19; 15:6-8; 16:1-21; 17:1; 20:1-3

2. Comparison of the historical events accompanying the destruction of Jerusalem in A.D. 70 with the related biblical prophecies (see also question #11).

3. Comparison of the lawlessness and anti-Christian attitudes that have prevailed throughout the ages with those of the end times.

## CREATIVE PROJECTS

1. Prepare a newspaper with imaginative articles about events of the end times.

2. Write a biographical profile of a "false prophet" of the end times who says he is the Christ (see questions #1-3).

3. Project an imaginative interview between a radio/TV reporter with a roving microphone on Main Street and various citizens at the time of changes in the sun, moon, and stars. Write a dialogue of what the various people interviewed might say about the signs in the heavens.

4. Dramatize the reactions of priests/ministers/worshipers in the temple when the beast of the end times sets up the "abomination of desolation" (see questions #10 and #11).

5. Write a diary of an observer of events of the end times.

6. Conduct a panel discussion on seductive methods used to gain an extra-world feeling, such as drugs, the occult, witchcraft, etc.

7. Write a paper on VALUES CLARIFICATION of various groups who live in the end time. What values, for instance, direct the activities of the following: (1) those who pose falsely as Christ; (2) those who remain true to Christ; (3) those who are seduced by false doctrine (see question #20)?

## GROUP DISCUSSION

What would you want to be doing when Christ returns? What kind of occupation would you like to be in? What recreation would you choose? What action should you take now?

# MILLENNIUM

## INDEPENDENT STUDY QUESTIONS

### Bible References

1. What is the chief source of information about the millennium in the Bible? What facts are revealed here? Revelation 20:2-7

2. What other Bible passages are considered references to this period of time? Micah 4:2,3; Isaiah 2:4; 11:6-9; 25:9

### Three Views

3. Explain the meaning of post-, a-, and pre-millennialism.

4. Both postmillennialism and amillennialism are hallmarked by a

symbolic interpretation of Scriptures relevant to the millennium. What arguments do proponents of these views use in defense of this kind of approach? Cite at least three Bible texts they might use to support their views. Colossians 1:13; 1 Thessalonians 2:12; Hebrews 12:28; Matthew 16:28

5. According to this symbolic approach, how is the "kingdom of God" to be understood? John 3:3-5; Matthew 18:3; Colossians 1:13,14

6. How would advocates of this method of interpretation understand the parables of the wheat and tares, the leaven, the mustard seed? Matthew 13:24-30, 31-33; 2 Peter 3:8,9

7. How would these optimistic advocates explain the great tribulation of the end times? The binding of Satan? Matthew 12:28,29; John 16:8,11; 12:31; Hebrews 2:14; Colossians 2:15. The first resurrection? Ephesians 2:1,5,6; Revelation 20:1-6

8. Postmillennarians and amillennarians would explain the regathering of Israel to Palestine not as a literal fulfillment of Old Testament prophecy, but as an "accident of history." What Scriptures do they use to support this explanation? Romans 10:11-13; Galatians 3:28,29; Isaiah 56:7,8

9. When does the resurrection of dead believers and the rapture of living believers take place according to these two views? 1 Corinthians 15:22-24; Matthew 25:31,32

10. How would they explain the following Old Testament prophecies:

a. God's promise to David that his throne would be established *forever*, not after the manner of men. 2 Samuel 7:16-19; Acts 2:29-36

b. Jerusalem as the capital of the kingdom. Isaiah 2:3; Hebrews 12:22,23; Galatians 4:26

c. Restoration of temple worship. Ezekiel 40-48

d. Israel promised a time of peace and rest. Isaiah 2:4; Micah 4:1,2; Romans 11:11,17; Acts 15:17

## History

11. Summarize briefly the history of millennialism.

12. Who are Gog and Magog? What is their relation to the millennium? Revelation 20:8; 1 Chronicles 1:5; 5:4; Ezekiel 38:2,3,14, 15,18; 39:1,6,11; Genesis 10:2

13. What time references are given for Gog's invasion of Israel?

Revelation 20:2-8; Ezekiel 38:8,11-13; 16; 39:27,28

14. Why do some Bible scholars identify Gog of Ezekiel with Gog of the Revelation? Ezekiel 38:22 and Revelation 20:9; Ezekiel 38:4 and Revelation 20:7,8; Ezekiel 38:6 and Revelation 20:8; Ezekiel 39:11 and Revelation 20:8; Ezekiel 38:8,14-16 and Revelation 20:7,8

## RESEARCH PAPERS

1. A history of denominations holding Premillennial, Amillennial, and Postmillennial views.

2. Israel and the millennium (Pre-, Post-, or A- viewpoints).

3. The first resurrection and the millennium.

4. The nature of the millennium.

5. St. Augustine's view of the millennium (or any other Bible scholar's).

6. The millennium and the final consummation.

7. A study of Gog and Magog.

## CREATIVE PROJECTS

The ideas listed under KINGDOM can also be used here.

1. Present a puppet show contrasting Antichrist's rule during the end times with Christ's during the millennium. Two puppet stages could be used if available, for contrast, one for Antichrist's kingdom on one side of the room, and one for Christ's on the other.

2. Write a dialogue between a wolf and a lamb living peaceably together in the millennium, contrasting their former with their present life style (see Isaiah 11).

3. Write a poem on the desert blossoming like a rose. For creative suggestions, though in reversal, see T. S. Eliot's *The Wasteland.*

4. Compose folk songs that might be sung during the millennium.

5. Create a cassette of selected mood music that speaks harmony, peace, and contentment, such as will characterize the millennium. Some comments or poetry might be inserted here and there.

6. Write a one-scene drama with birds as characters discussing the millennium. (You might get ideas from Chaucer's *Parliament of Foules* or Aristophanes' *Birds.*)

7. Prepare a magazine/journal/newspaper, such as might appear in the millennium.

8.  As a class project, the students could create an imaginary town of the millennium, in any part of the earth, write descriptions of it and of its citizens, explain its government and problems, publish an edition of its newspaper, design its school system and recreational opportunities, etc.

9.  For all of the prophetic themes — Antichrist, Armageddon, Kingdom, Millennium, etc. — students can write cinquains:

    1st line — one word names the topic — *kingdom*
    2nd line — two words define or describe the topic — *peace* and
        *plenty*
    3rd line — three words relate action — *giving, loving,* and *caring*
    4th line — four words reveal personal attitude — *fulfilled people*
        *ever growing*
    5th line — one word gives synonym for the topic — *Utopia*

## GROUP DISCUSSION

Since all Christians, living or dead, will partake of the first resurrection, they will live during the millennium. What sort of occupation, position, job would you like to be trusted with in Christ's kingdom? Are you preparing yourself now to be qualified for it then?

# RAPTURE

## INDEPENDENT STUDY QUESTIONS

### Pre-Tribulation Rapture

1.  When did the pre-tribulation rapture interpretation first come into existence?

2.  The pre-tribulation viewpoint is based on three major arguments, under which all other arguments can be categorized. Name these three.

3.  What biblical passages are cited in support of the argument that the great tribulation of the end times relates to Israel, not the Church? Jeremiah 30:6,7; Zechariah 13:8,9; Revelation 12

4.  Why do pre-tribbers believe that the nature of the Christian Church forbids its going through the great tribulation? Revelation 3:10; Romans 5:9

## Mid- and Post-Tribulation Rapture

5. How do mid- and post-tribbers respond to this argument of the pre-tribbers? What biblical references do they cite to support their belief that the Church is not exempt from tribulation? Acts 14:22; 1 Thessalonians 3:4; Revelation 1:9

6. What Bible verses refer to Christ coming a second time *for* His saints? 1 Thessalonians 4:13-17; Revelation 14:14,15. Returning after that *with* His saints? Jude 14; Revelation 19:11-14. Does the Bible state what time interval exists between these two events?

7. Which happens first when Christ returns — the resurrection of the dead in Christ or the levitation of the living saints? 1 Thessalonians 4:13-17

8. When does the resurrection of Old Testament believers take place? Daniel 12:1,2,13; Revelation 11:18

9. What events precede the rapture? 2 Thessalonians 2:1-5

10. What is the relation of the "firstfruits" to the main "harvest"? What is the relation of both to the "vintage"? Revelation 14. When do these events take place in relation to the destruction of Antichrist and his anti-Christian kingdom? Revelation 15-18

11. According to Daniel 12:1,2, and 13, Daniel himself will be resurrected *after* the great tribulation of the end times. How long will the great tribulation last, according to Daniel? Daniel 12:7. What triggered its beginning? Daniel 9:27. What other Bible verses refer to this exact time period? Revelation 11:2,3; 12:6,14; 13:5

## RESEARCH PAPERS

1. A history of the Pre-Tribulation Rapture Position.

2. A study of the Greek words referring to Christ's Second Coming.

3. The resurrection of Old Testament believers.

4. Events occurring *when* Christ returns.

5. Relation of the seventh and last trumpet and the Second Coming.

## CREATIVE PROJECTS

1. Present one of the current films available on the pre-trib rapture.

2. Write the scenario for a post-trib rapture film.

3. Conduct a three-way "debate" by proponents of the three different positions on the rapture.

4. Give or write book reviews, one each on a pre-, mid-, post-trib position.

## GROUP DISCUSSION

What would you want to be found doing when Christ returns in a moment, in the twinkling of an eye, as the lightning shines from the East to the West? Is there anything you would not like to be caught doing? What business would you like finished so as to present to Him good works? What actions are you taking to accomplish that goal?

# RESTORATION OF ISRAEL

## INDEPENDENT STUDY QUESTIONS

1. List the promises of restoration given to Israel in the Old Testament. List the things that are promised. Isaiah 11:11; Jeremiah 31:17; 32:41,42; 16:14,15; 23:3; 24:6-9; Ezekiel 37:25; Amos 9:14,15; Zechariah 10:10

2. What are the stated conditions of Israel's restoration? Deuteronomy 30:2-5; Jeremiah 17:24-27; 18:7-10; 22:1-5

3. Why does God pass by the conditions? Ezekiel 36:21-24,32 (also Isaiah 43:25; Ezekiel 20:9,14,17,22,33-44)

4. What will be the effect of Israel's restoration on the Gentiles? Isaiah 49:22,23; 60:10; Micah 7:16

5. What will be the *geographical* effect on Palestine? Isaiah 11:14-16; 27:12; 35:1,2,7; 65:8-10; Joel 3:18,19; Amos 9:12; Obadiah 18-20; Zephaniah 2:7. The *political* effect? Isaiah 11:13,14; 60:3-9,12,16; Jeremiah 30:21; Jeremiah 3:18; 23:5-8; 30:9; Ezekiel 34:23; 37:22,24-28. The *social* changes? Hosea 2:18; Jeremiah 31:14; Ezekiel 36:33-36; Micah 4:4; Isaiah 4:2; 29:17; 30:23-25; 35:10; 51:3,11. The *religious* changes? Isaiah 33:24; 60:21; Jeremiah 3:15-17; 23:4; 30:22; Ezekiel 36:33; 37:26; Joel 2:28,29

## RESEARCH PAPERS

1. A brief history of Israel in captivity for over 2,500 years.

2. A history of Israel(ites) in Palestine.

3. Arab-Israel animosities.

4. Prophecies on Israel's restoration.

5. An inquiry into the symbolic interpretation of Israel's restoration to the land.

6. Israel and the Christ.

## CREATIVE PROJECTS

1. Write a drama or present tableaux or musicals on the *four Jerusalems*:

    a. *Historical Jerusalem:* (1) the Jerusalem of the Jews, destroyed by the Babylonians and rebuilt by returning refugees.

    b. *Historical Jerusalem*: (2) where Jesus began His mission of redemption, where He suffered and died.

    c. *Prophetic Jerusalem*: (3) of the end times when two witnesses shall declare God's truth in an anti-Christian world kingdom.

    d. *Eternal Jerusalem*: (4) the new Jerusalem coming down out of heaven, prepared by God, an eternal city for the redeemed.

2. Draw (or collect) a series of maps on Israel's acquisition of land from the days of Joshua's conquest to the present.

3. Draw maps on natural resources in the Mideast. Locate oil, water reserves, arable land, and rainfall.

4. Present a travelog of Palestine.

5. Conduct a Jewish or Arab "bazaar" with booths, selling typical artifacts, gathered or created by the class.

6. Create a class "kibbutz," describing roles of each citizen, goals of the group, methods to increase motivation and productivity, and protection against guerrilla attacks.

7. Present one of the movies available on Palestine, such as Billy Graham's *His Land* or *The Exodus* or *Rosebud*.

8. Some Christian groups interpret the exile and return of the Jews as a symbol of mankind, unredeemed and redeemed. Examine how some Christian hymns spiritualize Israel into the Church:

    O Zion, Haste
    Hail to the Brightness of Zion's Glad Morning
    O Come, O Come, Emmanuel
    Triumphant Zion
    When, His Salvation Bringing

## GROUP DISCUSSION

Suppose you were an Arab who had been dispossessed of his home and land in one of the Arab-Israeli conflicts, and suppose you have been forced to live hand-to-mouth in a temporary settlement heavily "protected" by Israeli guards, and suppose that in the meantime you have become the only Christian in your family and among your relatives — what would you now do to improve your position?

# RESURRECTION

## INDEPENDENT STUDY QUESTIONS

### Two Resurrections

1. What is the difference between the two resurrections mentioned in the Bible? John 5:28,29; Luke 14:13,14; Hebrews 11:35; Philippians 3:10,11

2. What is the order of those resurrected? 1 Corinthians 15:23-25; Revelation 20:4-6, 11-15

### Participants

3. What is the nature of the resurrected body? 1 Corinthians 15:23-25; John 20:17, 19-27; Luke 13:30; 24:36-53

4. Who are the participants of the first resurrection? Revelation 20; 1 Thessalonians 4:13-18

5. Give some examples of those living in the Old Testament who believed in the resurrection. Hebrews 11:19; 1 Kings 17; 2 Kings 4:32-35; 13:20,21; Job 19:25-27; Psalms 16:10; 17:15; Isaiah 26:19; Daniel 12:1-3

6. How many witnesses saw Jesus after His resurrection? John 20:11-31; 21:1; Luke 24:13; 1 Corinthians 15:4-8

### Symbolic Use

7. How is the physical resurrection used by the Bible to refer symbolically to the normal life style of the Christian? Romans 6 and 7

## RESEARCH PAPERS

1. The doctrine of soul sleep held by some.

2. The time and events of the resurrection.

3. Resurrection power in the Christian life (Rom. 6:4,5).

4. Comparative study of Freudian concept of life-urge and death-wish in man with the Apostle Paul's "old man" and "new man."

5. Description of (an)other religion(s)'s belief in life after death.

## CREATIVE PROJECTS

1. Present a slide show, or give show-and-tell demonstrations, of a collection of famous art pictures on the crucifixion, analyzing their content, author's or painter's intention (where available), its faithfulness in representation of the biblical text, etc.

2. Death and resurrection are used in the Bible, not only to refer literally to physical states, but also to refer symbolically to spiritual states. Fold an 8½ x 11 sheet of paper lengthwise into two columns. At the top of the first column, write DEATH; at the top of the second column, write RESURRECTION LIFE. Under each column, list what the Bible says symbolically about each state. Romans 6; 7; 8:6; 1 Corinthians 15:21,26,54-56; 2 Corinthians 1:9; 7:10; Hebrews 2:9,15; 1 John 5:16,17; Revelation 2:11; 20:6,14; 21:4,8

3. Collect records on great musical compositions on Christ's resurrection. Prepare accompanying biographical and historical notes on the author and the composition. Or lead the class in singing some of the great resurrection songs and hymns.

4. Compose a poem or song on the resurrection life.

5. Write a *haiku* on the resurrection of spring out of a dead winter.

6. The psychologist Freud has pointed out that people can be subject to conflict between two forces inside themselves: a creative life-urge and a destructive death-wish. List twenty creative life-urges and twenty destructive death-wishes.

## GROUP DISCUSSION

Death-wishes take various forms: resentment, apathy, hate, lethargy, slothfulness, indolence, laziness, despair, cynicism. Recall five times when you were tempted in these directions. How did you overcome the temptation? How long did it take until you overcame the death-feeling indulgence? Volunteers may share their findings with the group.

# SECOND COMING

## INDEPENDENT STUDY QUESTIONS

### Bible References

1. Draw a chart on the four main Greek words used in the Bible for Christ's Second Coming, and list in parallel columns the content of each, emphasizing similarities and differences. Example:

| ἔφχομαυ "coming" | ἁποκδλυψις "revelation" | ἐπιΦδνειδ "manifestation" | πδφουνια "presence" |
|---|---|---|---|
| Sudden and unexpected Matt. 24:39, 42-44 | | | As lightning visible to all Matt. 24:27, 37-39 |
| After the great tribulation Matt.24:29,30 | Brings relief to saints suffering from tribulation 2 Thess. 1:7 | | |
| In judgment, reward, and punishment Matt. 25:31,32 | Day of Wrath and judgment 1 Peter 1:7; 4:13 | Judgments on Antichrist. Rewards to believers 2 Tim. 4:8; 1 Tim. 6:14 | Antichrist judged 2 Thess. 2:8 |

### Events When Christ Returns

2. What "signs" precede His coming? 2 Thessalonians 2:3; Matthew 24:14; Luke 21:25-27; Mark 13:7,8; Revelation 14:6,7; 2 Timothy 3:1-5

3. Describe how He will come again. Acts 1:9-11; Matthew 16:27; Revelation 19:11-16

4. What is the relation of His coming to the last trumpet? 1 Thessalonians 4:16; 1 Corinthians 15:52; Revelation 11:15-18

5. What is the role of angels at His coming? Matthew 16:27; Matthew 25:31; 2 Thessalonians 1:7,8; Revelation 8-18

6. What does the Bible say about "clouds" in relation to His coming?

Matthew 26:64; Mark 13:26; 14:62; Luke 21:27; Revelation 14:14-16; 19:11; Acts 1:9-11

### Influence on the Present

7. How does Christ's Second Coming influence the Christian's attitude and actions? Luke 9:26; Philippians 3:20; 1 Corinthians 4:5; 1 Thessalonians 3:12,13; 5:4-9; Matthew 24:44-51; 1 Timothy 4:1,2; Hebrews 10:36-38; 1 John 2:28; John 14:1-3

8. How does His Second Coming affect non-believers? Revelation 22:15; 2 Thessalonians 2:10-12; 2 Peter 3:3-5

9. Summarize views of the Second Coming other than the literal one, and present the *pros* and *cons* for each position.

## CREATIVE PROJECTS

1. First John 3:2,3 reads: "When he shall appear, we shall be like him; for we shall see him as he is. And every man that hath this hope in him, purifieth himself, even as he is pure." List 25 ways of "purifying" oneself as a Christian. Example: To exercise LOVE more often and more authentically would certainly be a way of "purifying" oneself. List 25 ways of saying "I LOVE YOU."

2. The chief difference between the sane and the insane is that one retains HOPE and the other has given up in despair. In what ways does "the blessed hope" motivate a Christian in his activities and sustain him through frustration, trials, and suffering?

3. Judaism has an interesting ritual at its Passovers — an empty chair called the ELIJAH CHAIR, since there was an Old Testament promise of "Elijah" returning before Messiah comes. The Lutheran Church symbolically celebrates Christ's coming in an ADVENT WREATH.List ten ways you might remind yourself of His Second Coming.

4. Study the liturgy of the Advent Season in Catholic and Episcopalian churches (which weave together the first historical coming, the second eschatological coming and the symbolic meaning of Christ's coming into one tapestry).

5. Write a kind of "mystery play" on the entire "Christmas cycle": Preparation for His Coming; His arrival and rejection; His departure; His return to celebrate His marriage to the Church; His presiding over His Kingdom.

6. Write a poem or song or antiphony, anticipating His Coming — for the morning, for the busy day, for the evening. Suggestion:

Conclude each stanza or antiphon with *Alleluia,* the Church's most glorious expression of joy. Varieties of moods: celebration of fulfilled redemption; hope and anticipation; longing for release from suffering, exile or tribulation; awe and worship of the majestic King of Kings; lament of the unprepared, yet redeemed, Bride, the Church, and bright rejoicing at His cleansing and reception.

7. Write a "legend" about nature's redemption at His Second Coming — how the grip of the "dark night" and "winter death" is released to eternal springtime blossom of hope (see Rom. 8:19-22).

8. Write a shortened form of the Medieval drama EVERYMAN to be presented in an evening church service. Remember the theme is "How can I be redeemed from everlasting death?"

## GROUP DISCUSSION

In the Apostle's Creed, we recite our faith collectively. Part of that creed states:

> I believe in God the Father Almighty, Maker of heaven and earth: and in Jesus Christ His only Son: our Lord, who was conceived by the Holy Ghost, born of the Virgin Mary, suffered under Pontius Pilate, was crucified, dead, and buried. . . the third day He rose again from the dead; He ascended into heaven and sitteth on the right hand of God the Father Almighty; from whence He shall come to judge the quick and the dead. . . .

What does our Lord Jesus' historical first coming mean to me? Do I pattern my life on His? List ten things He did that changed my attitudes or actions. How does the prophecy of His Second Coming affect me? Is my life style different in any way because of this belief?

# TIMES OF THE GENTILES

## INDEPENDENT STUDY QUESTIONS

1. What event(s) characterize(s) the times of the Gentiles? Luke 21:24; Revelation 11:1,2

2. Compare and contrast the "fours" prophecies of the Old Testament, representing Gentile kingdoms ruling over Israel:

four metals (Dan. 2)
four worms (Joel 1:4; 2:25)
four horns (Zech. 1:18-21)

four judgments (Ezek. 14:21)
four families (Jer. 15:3,4)
four beasts (Dan. 7)

3. What is the relation of Daniel's prophecy of the seventy weeks to the four Gentile kingdoms? Daniel 9:27; cf. Daniel 2 and 7

4. What events mark the beginning of the times of the Gentiles? The end?

5. Describe the last three and a half years of the times of the Gentiles. Daniel 12:6,7; Revelation 11:2-11; 12:6,14; 13:5; 9:21;16:9,21; Revelation 8:7-12; 15; 16

## RESEARCH PAPERS

1. Comparative study of Old Testament prophecies of the four kingdoms of Gentile dominion.

2. The final phase of the times of the Gentiles.

3. Political history of the conquest of Jerusalem.

## CREATIVE PROJECTS

1. Prepare a chart of the Old Testament prophecies of the four Gentile kingdoms.

2. Write a short story or anecdote about some historical incident connected with the conquest of Jerusalem, such as the Crusades.

3. Write poetic laments such as Jews might chant at the Wailing Wall.

4. Prepare a slide show on the Wailing Wall, accompanying sound and music, giving historical background, present state, and future hope.

5. Make a study of hymns which refer to Jerusalem.

## GROUP DISCUSSION

The Jews lost Jerusalem when they gave up belief in God. In the prophetic future, God rewards believers with "a New Jerusalem," an eternal city prepared for them. Examine Christian hymns relating to the New Jerusalem: (1) State what elements refer to a literal city; (2) state what elements refer to a spiritual condition of the soul; (3) cite the Bible verses which suggested the words of the song to its composer.

Jerusalem the Golden
I Saw the Holy City
No Night There (in the "city foursquare")
O Mother Dear, Jerusalem
Jerusalem My Happy Home
We're Marching to Zion

# THE GREAT TRIBULATION

## INDEPENDENT STUDY QUESTIONS

### Bible References

1. How is the word "tribulation" (Greek - θλίψις) used in the Bible?
Matthew 24:21,29; 2 Corinthians 8:13; Philippians 4:14; John 16:21;
Colossians 1:24; 2 Peter 2:4; Revelation 7:14

### Time

2. Where does the phrase "the great tribulation" appear in the
Bible? Revelation 7:14. What is the time of this affliction?

3. What are the events described here as connected with "the great
tribulation"?

4. What other Bible verses refer to a great tribulation of the end
times? Daniel 12:1-4; 9:27; Matthew 24:15,21,22,29-35; Jeremiah
30:7

### Relation to Jew and Gentile

5. Why do Bible students emphasize Israel's connection with this
time of trouble? Jeremiah 30:7; Matthew 24:15; Daniel 12:1-4; Revelation 12

6. Which Bible references also describe this as a time of judgment
upon the Gentile nations for their rejection of Christ? Isaiah 26:21;
27; 34:1,2

## RESEARCH PAPERS

1. Relation of Israel to the great tribulation.
2. Relation of the Church to the great tribulation.
3. Details of the great tribulation in the Revelation.

4. The seven-sealed book and the great tribulation.

5. Biblical *terminus a quo* and *terminus ad quem* of the great tribulation.

6. Place of suffering in God's eternal purpose according to the Bible.

## CREATIVE PROJECTS

1. Categorize the 54 uses of the word "tribulation" in the New Testament.

2. Write a review or give a report on Fox's *Book of Martyrs*.

3. List 25 ways in which we ourselves bring suffering on another person.

4. Role-play a member of a minority group. Give a fiery speech complaining about undeserved and unnecessary suffering inflicted by outside groups.

## GROUP DISCUSSION

Consider some expressed or smoldering complaints of various minority groups in the town. Discuss a Christian resolution to the conflicts. Discuss the nature of the conflicts:

    a. Different goals
    b. Different approaches to the same goal
    c. Different values
    d. Different needs, psychological or physical
    e. Differing role expectations